PENGUIN CLASSICS

THE ORIGIN OF THE FAMILY,
PRIVATE PROPERTY AND THE STATE

Friedrich Engels was born in Germany in 1820, the son of a textile manufacturer. After his military training in Berlin he became the Manchester agent of his father's business, and soon became immersed in Chartism and the problems of the urban proletariat newly created by the industrial revolution. In 1844 he wrote his famous *Condition of the Working Class in England*, and by 1848 he was a firm friend of Marx. Their ideas were incorporated into *The Communist Manifesto*, although the writing of the *Manifesto* itself was solely Marx's work. Engels provided Marx with money, and after 1870 spent all his time assisting him in his research. After Marx's death Engels continued his work on *Das Kapital*, and completed it in 1894, a year before his own death. His other works include *The Peasant War in Germany*, *Anti-Duhring* and *Socialism: Utopian and Scientific*.

•

Michèle Barrett was born in 1949 and teaches sociology at the City University, London. She is a member of the *Feminist Review* editorial collective and is the author of *Women's Oppression Today: Problems in Marxist Feminist Analysis* (1980), joint author, with Mary McIntosh, of *The Anti-social Family* (1982), and has written many articles and papers.

FRIEDRICH ENGELS

THE ORIGIN OF THE FAMILY, PRIVATE PROPERTY AND THE STATE

Introduction by Michèle Barrett

PENGUIN BOOKS

PENGUIN BOOKS

Published by the Penguin Group
Penguin Books Ltd, 27 Wrights Lane, London W8 5TZ, England
Penguin Books USA Inc., 375 Hudson Street, New York, New York 10014, USA
Penguin Books Australia Ltd, Ringwood, Victoria, Australia
Penguin Books Canada Ltd, 10 Alcorn Avenue, Toronto, Ontario, Canada M4V 3B2
Penguin Books (NZ) Ltd, 182–190 Wairau Road, Auckland 10, New Zealand

Penguin Books Ltd, Registered Offices: Harmondsworth, Middlesex, England

First published 1884
This edition of the text first published by Lawrence & Wishart 1972
Published with a new Introduction in Penguin Classics 1986
3 5 7 9 10 8 6 4

Printed in England by Clays Ltd, St Ives plc
Filmset in 10/12pt VIP Palatino

Contents

Introduction

It may seem strange to the contemporary reader that Engels's project, in *The Origin of the Family*, *Private Property and the State*, was to present the argument of a book that he had not himself read when he started to write. Even odder, perhaps, is the fact that the rather patchy and uneven result of this exercise was to become not only a classic text of the Marxist canon but also a blueprint for policies of women's emancipation in many countries of the world today. Although Engels's book has been criticized – some would say demolished – from every possible factual and theoretical angle conceived of in the century since it was written, it remains obstinately relevant and persistently discussed. This is because the questions that it raises are as far from being solved today as when Engels wrote, and because the answers he gave to them are still sufficiently plausible to be worth our serious attention.

Morgan, Marx and the Background of the Text

The story of the origin of *The Origin* begins in 1877 with the publication of *Ancient Society* by the early American anthropologist Lewis Henry Morgan. Subtitled *Researches in the Lines of Human Progress from Savagery through Barbarism to Civilization* the book attempted to construct a history of stages of social organization and of the family. Morgan argued several of the theses that were later to be articulated by Engels in *The Origin*, notably the relationship between the emergence of private property and the monogamous family form. *Ancient Society* also propounded the view that various anthropological 'anomalies' were easily explicable if one accepted that the early usual practice was to reckon kinship through descent from the mother rather than the father. Marx had a copy of Morgan's book and between 1880 and 1881 he copied and paraphrased large parts of it into a notebook, adding comments of his own. Although Marx himself did not write up these notes for publication they can be studied in their original form – characteristically expressed in a mixture of English, German and Latin – in the meticulous edition of *The Ethnological Notebooks of Karl Marx* produced by Lawrence Krader in 1972.[1] It seems that Marx's copy of the book was on loan, having been brought back from the United States by the ethnologist Maxim Kovalevsky, since Engels could not find it in Marx's library after his death in 1883.

Engels, having discovered Marx's lengthy abstract, was frustrated in his attempts to lay his hands on a copy of the book itself. In February 1884 he wrote a letter to Karl Kautsky in Zürich, revealing to posterity the astonishing speed with which *The Origin* was written, since it appeared a mere three months later in May 1884. He wrote:

There exists an *important* book on the condition of primitive society, as important as Darwin is in biology, and of course it is again Marx who discovered it: Morgan, *Ancient Society*, 1877. Marx spoke about it but my head was full of other things at that time and he never returned to it. This must have suited him for he *himself* wanted to publicize the book among the Germans, as I see from the quite extensive extracts he made. Morgan has quite independently discovered the Marxian materialist conception of history within the limits prescribed by his subject and he concludes with directly communist propositions in relation to present-day society . . . If I had the time I would work up the material, with Marx's notes, for a feature article in the *Sozialdemokrat* or the *Neue Zeit*, but that is out of the question.[2]

Engels added that he had ordered Morgan five weeks earlier but couldn't get it, and indeed when *The Origin*

1. *The Ethnological Notebooks of Karl Marx*, transcribed and ed. L. Krader (Van Gorcum & Co., Assen, Netherlands, 1972).
2. Letter to Karl Kautsky, 16 February 1884.

appeared three months later he was still complaining – this time in a note to the Preface – that Morgan was unobtainable in London. (He eventually got a second-hand copy at the end of March.) As is clear from his preface to the fourth edition of *The Origin*, written in 1891, Engels tended to view the difficulty of obtaining Morgan's book as a symptom of attempts by rival schools of anthropological thought to silence and suppress Morgan's discoveries.

Meanwhile, however, Engels must have decided that he did have the time to work up Marx's notes for publication. Reading Morgan now, it is interesting to see how Engels drew from it not merely the raw material but also the main arguments of the historical theory he propounded in *The Origin*. In fact, the way in which Engels transformed the material was by rendering it in a more political and theoretical form and by adding perceptive insights into the implications of Morgan's argument for contemporary marriage and family practices in advanced capitalism.

Let us look briefly at Morgan's treatment of the points that were to be taken up most forcefully by Engels. Morgan commented that the term 'family', stemming as it does from the Latin word for a servant, was not of great use in understanding ancient and prehistoric kinship arrangements. It was, he realized, a great error to assume that ancient kinship structures were made up of aggregations of modern 'families' and he argued that the reverse was true – that the modern family had developed from the larger, clannish, structures of the past. He argued that kinship, the notion of begetting and common descent, was most appropriately signified by the terms *gens* (Latin), *genos* (Greek) and *ganas* (Sanskrit) and he used the term *gens* as that most central to the analysis of kinship. He defined the *gens* as '. . . a body of consanguinei descended from the same common ancestor, distinguished by a gentile name, and bound together by affinities of blood'.[3]

3. Lewis Henry Morgan, *Ancient Society: Researches in the Lines of Human Progress from Savagery through Barbarism to Civilization* (Meridian Books, New York, 1963), p. 62.

Morgan's contribution to early anthropology was to challenge what we might now regard as a 'patriarchal' assumption. He tried to prove that although most societies now tended to calculate descent through the father's side, in an earlier period the usual practice had been to reckon descent from the mother. In modern anthropological terms he was arguing that matrilineality had been the norm and patrilineal societies had developed later. For obvious biological reasons it is easier to be sure of the identity of a child's mother than of that of its father and Morgan thought that in order to bring about the change to a much more difficult system of kinship there would have needed to be a substantial motive. This motive he identified as property. It was only, wrote Morgan, when a move towards a more monogamous form of marriage was accompanied by the amassing of property (at first through the domestication of animals) that fathers began to see how unfair was a system that excluded their own children from inheritance. The motivation towards change came therefore from men, but only when the existence of individually held private property had given it a material basis. The modern family form is hence a result of this development. Morgan's thesis – as reproduced by Engels – can be summarized in the following extract from *Ancient Society*:

Where descent is in the female line, as it was universally in the archaic period, the gens is composed of a supposed female ancestor and her children, together with the children of her female descendants, through females, in perpetuity; and where descent is in the male line – into which it was changed after the appearance of property in masses – of a supposed male ancestor and his children, together with the children of his male descendants, through males, in perpetuity. The family name among ourselves is a survival of the gentile name, with descent in the male line, and passing in the same manner. The modern family, as expressed by its name, is an unorganized gens; with the bond of kin broken, and its members as widely dispersed as the family name is found.[4]

Morgan himself had spent a considerable amount of time with the Iroquois Indians of North America and was much

4. Morgan, loc. cit.

influenced by the favourable position of women in their society. His account of the development of family types insists that the schema he outlines, from consanguine and 'punaluan' forms of group marriage to the development of pairing marriage, which he describes as first syndyasmian/polygamous and then monogamian, is one in which male power increases. The archaic forms he associates with societies where female power necessarily reigns – hence the expression 'the matriarchal gens'. The idea of 'primitive matriarchy' had been previously reinforced by Bachofen's much-referred-to text Das Mutterrecht ('Mother-right').[5] Morgan tends to use the word 'gyneocracy' to refer to women's power, but it is clear that he shares, at least to some degree, Bachofen's perception of ancient society as matriarchal. In this, of course, Engels follows Morgan and we shall see later how Engels translates the supposed shift from matrilineal to patrilineal kinship into what he calls the 'world-historic defeat of the female sex'.

A further point to be noted from Morgan's Ancient Society is the emphasis placed on the origin of government. It would be wrong to think, as is commonly assumed, that Morgan was concerned only with the family and kinship and that Engels welded the material into a consideration of relations between family and state in class society. Nearly 350 pages, the largest section of Morgan's book, are devoted to a general heading 'Growth of the Idea of Government', and this precedes in Morgan the discussion of the theory of stages of family forms and that of the rise of private property. It is not without interest that in his notes Marx reversed the order of sections in Ancient Society so that the government section fell at the end rather than towards the beginning of the book.[6] Morgan's sequence government–family–property thus reads in Marx's notebook family–property–government, and Marx's reorganization reflects his tendency to accept the conventional view of 'the family' as the most elementary unit of

5. See the selection of writings in J. J. Bachofen, Myth, Religion and Mother-Right (Routledge & Kegan Paul, London, 1968).
6. See The Ethnological Notebooks, p. 11.

society. In this sense it could be argued that Morgan had done rather more of Engels's theoretical as well as empirical groundwork than is often supposed by those who imagine that Morgan provided the data and Engels the interpretation.

I make this point because it is important to understand that Engels's text *The Origin of the Family, Private Property and the State* began as the very modest project of making available to a wider readership the research – thought by Engels to be important and controversial in its implications – of a neglected anthropologist. He wanted, however, to do so in such a way as to draw out these implications from his own point of view. As he was finishing it in April 1884 he wrote to Kautsky, 'There would be no point in writing it if I merely wanted to give an "objective" report on Morgan without treating him critically, without utilizing the new results and presenting them in connection with our views and the conclusions already reached.'[7] But we must remember that this critical treatment was intended to be an article or pamphlet, rather than a monograph or book. It was published the following month in Zürich and there can be no doubt that it was written in a hurry. Modern scholars are surprised to encounter Engels's final footnote, which begins as follows: 'I originally intended to place the brilliant criticism of civilization which is scattered through the work of Charles Fourier beside that of Morgan and my own. Unfortunately, I have not the time . . .' (p. 216). Engels did, however, make extravagant claims for the significance of Morgan's discoveries, regarding him as a Darwin or Marx in his own field and claiming (in 1891) that new evidence had left all the major lines of Morgan's work still in command of the field. Yet it must still come as a surprise that what is, despite patches of extraordinary perceptiveness, a rather unscholarly and speculative book, was immediately hailed as an authoritative work. Certainly the book hit a nerve of contemporary interest, for reasons that I shall return to later, and, although not translated into English until the 1902 American edition, went through many reprints and several European translations soon after

7. Letter to Karl Kautsky, 26 April 1884.

its first publication. Its canonization within the Marxist tradition was soon secure, though perhaps it was just as well that Marx had died the year before, since one can only surmise what he would have said about it. By 1919 the reputation of Engels's *The Origin* was sealed in Lenin's lavish, indeed rash, praise: 'This is one of the fundamental works of modern socialism, every sentence of which can be accepted with confidence, in the assurance that it has not been said at random but is based on immense historical and political material.'[8]

It must be said that in some respects the text is not really equal to the weight of deference that has been loaded upon it, and this mismatch between the text itself and its history and influence is rather odd. Flawed and disputed as it is, it has called forth a vast range of adverse comments, many of them justified. Yet such is the significance of the issues that Engels is dealing with – and especially so since the revival of feminism and the attempt to develop a distinctively 'socialist-feminist' perspective – that the book remains of much more than historical interest. Let us consider first the different points of view from which *The Origin* has been criticized.

Critical Discussion of Engels's Text

Perhaps the most fundamental criticisms of Engels come from those anthropologists who reject his account as resting, quite simply, on errors. (The text also contains statements that are incorrect in terms of modern scientific knowledge, for example the remarks about brain size on p. 55.) Following Morgan, Engels saw the period they called 'savagery' (that of hunter/gatherer societies) as one in which, since food for subsistence was directly appropriated by both men and women from nature, there was an equality between men and women at the heart of the social arrangements. It is in this early period that the matrilineal kinship systems flourished, embodying women's general power in these societies. It is

8. Lenin, *Collected Works*, Vol. 30, p. 473.

with the development of food cultivation and the domestication of animals – in societies that Morgan and Engels categorize under 'barbarism' and that we would call horticultural/pastoral – that a division of labour between men and women arises in a significant form. Engels casts the earlier period in terms of a supposed 'natural' division of labour between men and women, but this is considerably more than the division of labour in human reproductive biology. The following passage is an example of this tendency in Engels towards generalization and reading the past in terms of subsequent history:

With the herds and the other new riches, a revolution came over the family. To procure the necessities of life had always been the business of the man; he produced and owned the means of doing so. The herds were the new means of producing these necessities; the taming of the animals in the first instance and their later tending were the man's work. To him, therefore, belonged the cattle and to him the commodities and the slaves received in exchange for cattle [p. 199].

The Danish anthropologist Peter Aaby has succinctly objected to this proposed sequence of events. In the first place, he points out, women were probably responsible for the largest share of food production in hunter/gatherer societies; secondly, in many societies the development of herds did not precede the growth of horticulture, and women would probably have controlled the resource of crops, which would be as significant as controlling animals.[9] Two British feminist anthropologists, Kate Young and Olivia Harris, find equally basic anthropological errors in the account Engels puts forward: they argue that a survey of hunter/gatherer societies does not support the idea that there is a link between this form of production and a favourable status for women. They also point out that *matrilineal* systems are ones in which inheritance goes from a man to his sister's son (a very different matter from going from mother to daughter), and

9. Peter Aaby, 'Engels and women', *Critique of Anthropology*, Vol. 3, nos. 9/10 (1977), pp. 27–8.

hence to see matriliny as a residual form of matriarchal social organization is dubious.[10] The American anthropologist Judith K. Brown, reviewing the evidence about the Iroquois on which much of the Morgan/Engels theory rests, concludes as follows:

> The unusual role of Iroquois women in politics, religion and domestic life cannot be dismissed simply as a historical curiosity. It cannot be explained by Iroquois kinship structure, nor can it be attributed to the size of women's contribution to Iroquois subsistence. The powerful position of Iroquois women was the result of their control over the economic organization of their tribe.[11]

These authors, and many more who could be cited in addition, stand on one side of a debate that has run for some time now on the status of the evidence and arguments used by Morgan and Engels. On the other side stand anthropologists such as Eleanor Leacock, who has written a substantial introduction to a previous edition of *The Origin*,[12] and Evelyn Reed, the author of *Woman's Evolution: From Matriarchal Clan to Patriarchal Family*.[13] The debate harks back to the fundamental controversy that has dominated anthropology since the nineteenth century as to whether the earliest forms of human social organization were patriarchal or matriarchal in character (or whether it is necessarily impossible to say). Thorny and contentious as these issues may be, they are straightforward and clear as daylight in comparison with the critiques of Engels that hinge on theoretical and methodological disputes rather than on the supposed 'facts' of history and prehistory.

10. Kate Young and Olivia Harris, 'The subordination of women in cross-cultural perspective' in Mary Evans (ed.), *The Woman Question* (Fontana, London, 1982). p. 468.

11. Judith K. Brown, 'Iroquois women: an ethnohistoric note' in Rayna R. Reiter (ed.), *Toward an Anthropology of Women* (Monthly Review Press, New York, 1975), p. 251.

12. Frederick Engels, *The Origin of the Family, Private Property and the State*, with an Introduction and notes by Eleanor Burke Leacock (Lawrence & Wishart, London, 1972).

13. Evelyn Reed, *Woman's Evolution: From Matriarchal Clan to Patriarchal Family* (Pathfinder, New York, 1975).

One way to approach these criticisms is to look at one of the most general objections levelled against the type of work that *The Origin* represents – evolutionary anthropology. Morgan's division of human history into 'savagery' and 'barbarism' (with three stages apiece) preceding 'civilization' reflects a belief that societies can usefully be described in such sweeping terms and, perhaps more significantly, that history represents an inexorable march of progress – an evolution towards higher forms of social life. Both of these beliefs are radically disputed, within and beyond anthropology. The exercise known as 'periodization' is fraught with problems in that even supposedly 'primitive' societies frequently do not fit the rigid specifications given in schemes such as Morgan's. Also, as several critical commentators have noted, Morgan draws up his classification of the stages of human development on the basis largely of the Iroquois, aboriginal Australians and the Greeks and Romans, with a few passing references to Scottish clans and so on. This leaves at least two continents ignored, and obviously the majority of the world's societies are not taken into account in any serious way. In addition, it is often the case that schemes such as these tend to judge the past according to the present, to see the present as a plumbline against which other periods are measured – and probably found wanting.

The desire to arrange history and prehistory into stages carries with it an almost inevitable set of value judgements about progress. Morgan himself is rather careful not to fall into this trap too easily, and he offers an interesting discussion, headed 'The ratio of human progress', in which he argues that some of the earliest developments were more momentous than the great leaps and bounds by which 'civilization' has advanced.[14] Nevertheless his world-view is a strongly evolutionist one, of the kind which has been extensively criticized and for the most part rejected since that time. Yet although evolutionist arguments have little credibility nowadays as explanations of social change, certain traces of this view of the world retain an influence in

14. *Ancient Society*, pp. 37–8.

Marxism, and one which it has proved difficult to reject without also losing the notion of a future socialist society. The Italian Marxist philosopher Sebastiano Timpanaro has shown the extent to which Marxist thought in general rests on these nineteenth-century ideas of progress through increasing control over nature – an evolutionary 'triumphalism' that stresses human capacity rather than the obstacles provided by the natural world.[15]

There can be no doubt that Marx and Engels shared this moral universe, though in the case of kinship and marriage arrangements their view was more complex – they hoped for a transcended version of the earlier form with greater equality. Engels ends *The Origin* with a quotation from Morgan about a future democratic society. It will be, he writes, 'a revival, in a higher form, of the liberty, equality and fraternity of the ancient gentes'. August Bebel makes more of this passage from the point of view of a rather utopian forecast of the position of women. Under socialism, he predicted, 'Now woman again fills the active *rôle* that once was hers in primitive society. She does not become the mistress, she is the equal of man.'[16]

Allied to this evolutionary perspective are a series of profound difficulties with the type of evidence that Morgan and Engels rely on. It is a mark of their methodological innocence that they can on occasion quote the letters of people such as missionaries as sources of information rather than as opinions to be considered. They have a complete confidence – entirely characteristic of the nineteenth-century Western European mind that saw itself quite a way up the human hierarchy – in their own judgements and interpretations of other cultures. Although Morgan lived with the Iroquois himself, some of what he wrote, and all of what Engels wrote, was a mixture of second-hand observation and speculation that is riddled with problems. Liz Brown, arguing against the attempts of anthropologists to 'modernize' Engels

15. Sebastiano Timpanaro, *On Materialism* (Verso, London, 1980).
16. August Bebel, *Woman under Socialism*, trans. Daniel de Leon (New York Labor News Company, New York, 1904), p. 348.

by correcting the errors of fact in his text, stresses that *The Origin* is a text with a history. It is implicated in a particular theory, a specific view of the status of ethnographic evidence, a particular set of assumptions about what constitutes the 'facts'.[17] Without accepting that any work of this kind must necessarily be a textual phenomenon to explain rather than a source of knowledge for us, it is nevertheless true that the area of interpretation is extremely wide in *The Origin*. What kind of methodological problems arise with Engels's treatment of the material?

The first point to raise concerns Morgan's explanation of the conundrum that set off a great part of his work: why was it that systems of consanguinity did not match actual family practices? He found the Iroquois in (roughly) pairing marriage, but using a kinship terminology appropriate to group (cross-cousin) marriage; he found in Hawaii a group whose actual practice fitted Iroquois terminology but whose own language of consanguinity was yet more open in that it did not distinguish between siblings and cousins. Morgan's conclusion, accepted by Engels as it had been by Marx, was that family and marriage practices, being dynamic, moved on while languages of consanguinity ossified until some great upheaval forced a change. Such terminologies, then, teach us what went before; they act as a kind of fossil record of previous family forms. If this is accepted – which it certainly need not be – many consequences follow. It is instructive to read the text with this assumption in mind, for in many instances both Morgan and Engels deduce the existence of something solely on this basis.

Engels defends this procedure quite militantly, claiming that the deduction of a family form from a system of consanguinity is just as certain as the deduction of an animal's existence from a bone of its skeleton. Furthermore, in his preface to the fourth edition he argues, against the charges of those who have suggested that Morgan's systems of consanguinity could be codes of politeness, that codes such

17. Liz Brown, 'The family and its genealogies – a discussion of Engels' "Origin of the Family" ', *m/f a feminist journal*, no. 3 (1979), pp. 11–13.

as the use of 'brother' and 'sister' in the labour movement do not render meaningless the family referents of those terms. Yet Engels does not really engage with the problem; he does not accept that language could exist as other than a reflection of some 'real' social practice such as the family and hence he cannot see how dangerous the process of deduction is. It is clear from Marx's comment (quoted in *The Origin*, p. 60) on this notion of kinship terminology lagging behind changes in family practices – '. . . the same is true of the political, juridical, religious, and philosophical systems in general' – that such phenomena were seen from the point of view of a theory of ideology which regards them as only reflections of economic and social reality.

The second major methodological point is of particular relevance to feminism, for it concerns Morgan's and Engels's interpretation of the status of women in different societies. They are arguing that in general the position of women is better in societies whose family form allows them more freedom than the double standard of monogamy (double because imposed only on the women, in order to secure legitimate heirs for men) characteristic of class societies. Hence they repeatedly argue that forms of marriage such as cross-cousin, or, more generally, group marriage (one particular form being referred to by Morgan as 'punaluan') were relatively egalitarian as between men and women. It is worth looking in some detail at one or two examples of how they interpret data, since we shall see that Engels in particular has a tendency to see only what he wants to see.

Perhaps the most striking case is the addendum entitled 'A Recently Discovered Case of Group Marriage', which is the text of an article published by Engels in 1892, confirming the argument of *The Origin*. Engels introduces the ethnographic report from the island of Sakhalin by describing the family form in the following terms: '. . . a man is married to all the wives of his brothers and to all the sisters of his wife, which means, seen from the woman's side, that his wife may freely practise sexual intercourse with the brothers of her husband and the husbands of her sisters' (p. 218). But does it mean this? When we look at the actual report, what it says is, 'To this day *every Gilyak has the rights of a husband in regard to the wives of his brothers and to the sisters of his wife*; at any rate, the exercise of these rights is not regarded as impermissible' (p. 219). There is no mention of the woman's sexual rights, and our suspicions might well be confirmed by passages such as, 'When a Gilyak dies, his wife passes by decision of the gens to one of his brothers . . .' (p. 220). Of course it is quite possible that the western ethnographer who compiled the report imposed a sexist reading upon what he found and did not report it accurately, but the plain fact is that Engels could not have proved this with any certainty and had himself no more to draw on than the report itself. However, before we jump to a purist critique of this unjustified inference on Engels's part we would do well to remember how rare it is for modern male anthropologists – let alone nineteenth-century ones – to consider sexuality from the woman's point of view. Credit should surely go to such well-intentioned attempts.

Morgan does quote information on the punaluan family that suggests equality – for example Dr Bartlett's ideologically suffused comment about the Sandwich Islands: 'The natives had hardly more modesty or shame than so many animals. Husbands had many wives, and wives many husbands, and exchanged with each other at pleasure.'[18] However, many of Morgan's other sources seem less credible as support for his theory. His treatment of the well-known reference in Caesar to the Ancient Britons ('. . . by tens and twelves, husbands possessed their wives in common . . .') is, although rather engaging, so implausible that Engels sensibly ignores it in his discussion of this passage from *Ancient Society*. Morgan writes: 'The correlative group which this presupposes, where several sisters shared their husbands in common, is not suggested directly by Caesar; but it probably existed as the complement of the first.'[19] This is completely fanciful, but not untypical in the way it reveals profound methodological

18. Morgan, *Ancient Society*, p. 436.
19. Morgan, op. cit., p. 439.

problems and what we must now regard as unsatisfactory standards of scholarship.

Morgan and Engels were both concerned to strip away some of the Victorian sexual hypocrisy, and the sexism, that surrounded ethnography and travellers' accounts, but it is possible that they went too far in their re-interpretation of previous sources. It is interesting, for example, that Engels so dislikes Bachofen's term 'hetaerism' as a description of what he and Morgan call group marriage, for then as now the term carried strong overtones of concubinage and prostitution which Engels found unacceptable, but which might of course not be unreasonable. Perhaps the most extraordinary instance of the consequences of this style of analysis are the comments on the supposed residue of punaluan marriage customs in the conventional 'right' of particular men to women as brides, permanent or temporary. Morgan discusses this in relation to a practice among some North American Indians of regarding a man married to an eldest daughter as entitled to the sisters of his wife as wives when they reach marriageable age. This he sees as a 'genuine survival of the ancient punaluan custom', albeit one difficult to operationalize.[20] Engels gives a more dramatic example, succeeding in casting a politically rosy glow over the offensive practice of *jus primae noctis*. He writes: 'Among the Scots, as among the Welsh, a relic even of the punaluan family persisted into the Middle Ages in the form of the right of the first night which the head of the clan or the king, as last representative of the former community of husbands, had the right to exercise with every bride, unless it was compounded for money' (p. 170). From a feminist point of view this passage compares unfavourably with Engels's treatment, in *The Condition of the Working Class in England* (1844), of this seigneurial custom when it came to manufacturers sexually exploiting the young women they employed.[21] It seems extraordinary that the unintended consequence of the appropriation of Morgan's theory should,

20. Morgan, op. cit., p. 441.

21. Frederick Engels, *The Condition of the Working Class in England* (Lawrence & Wishart, London, 1973), p. 165.

effectively, be a complete denial of women's oppression in pre-monogamous marriage. No explanation, other than the general theory of a patriarchal takeover, is given as to why these male rights and privileges alone should survive, and the effect of the argument must surely be to exculpate men.

This point would, however, be contested by those feminists who support the Morgan/Engels thesis on the history of family forms. Underlying the debate is an interesting set of questions about female sexuality, and Eleanor Leacock challenges a number of prejudices in her fascinating defence of the esquimo practice whereby a visitor would sleep with an unattached woman or the host's wife. Leacock says that to regard this practice as symptomatic of the low status of women would be ethnocentric, since it would be presuming that women only enjoyed sex with their husbands and did not care for variety.[22] Yet what this glosses over, and what is glossed over in both Engels and Morgan, is the question of *choice*. What practice provides company for the travelling esquimo woman? Who decides which woman is to sleep with the visiting man? Why is the notion of sexual 'rights' found only in relation to men and not to women? To what extent in this ethnographic data, and indeed in Engels's formulation of Morgan's position, is woman ever presented as a sexual subject with desires of a status comparable to that of male desires (which are usually construed as 'natural')? It must be conceded that by the lights of contemporary feminism the equality between the sexes that is evoked is an extremely limited one.

At this point it is necessary to bring up to date the critical commentary on *The Origin* and raise questions about the bearing Engels's text has had on developments since its publication in 1884. Here three main topics present themselves: the changing character of the state; the transformation of both the bourgeois and the proletarian forms of family; and the position and emancipation of women. As far as the state is concerned, it is important to note that Engels's book

22. See Eleanor Leacock's Introduction to *The Origin of the Family, Private Property and the State* (Lawrence & Wishart, London, 1972), p. 31.

is not about 'the family'; it concerns itself with the emergence of the state in class society as it is related to monogamous marriage. His view of the state is straightforward and represents the classic position in Marxist thought: the state is, *tout court*, there to protect the interests of the owners of private property. His summary of the institution that was 'wanting' as property came to be amassed identified the following needs: to secure individual riches; to sanctify private property; to endow social recognition on new methods of property acquisition; to perpetuate class cleavage and exploitation (p. 141). The state was the solution to these problems and had to be invented. This representation of the state as the vehicle for the protection of bourgeois class interests is now regarded by many Marxist theorists as too simple, especially considering the significant changes in the role of the state during the past century. So locating and explaining the origin of the state in capitalist society does not necessarily resolve all the issues involved in the interpretation of the state in a later period.

It is not appropriate here to enter into the complex debates in Marxist theory as to the best way of characterizing the state in capitalist society, but it is relevant to draw attention to particular problems as they affect the argument about family forms. An obvious one is that of divorce: the extension to the working class of access to legal services previously only available to the rich has enabled considerable numbers of working-class people to share the privilege of being able to end marriage if they choose. Also the exclusive backing given by the law in the nineteenth century to the bourgeois man's rights and inheritance has been substantially modified by the considerable legislation providing for a more equitable division of marital property on divorce. There has been considerable discussion of the ways in which the state can be said to 'regulate' domestic life, and in this respect too the state plays a role that is broader than the representation of property interest.

One of the strengths of Engels's analysis is the way in which he specifies differences between marriage as between different social classes. As is well known, he argues that marriage in the proletariat is founded on 'individual sex love', where no economic considerations sully the relationship between husband and wife; among the bourgeoisie, by contrast, Engels holds that the requirements of property inheritance construct the relationship as one of prostitution. The bourgeois wife, he claims, 'only differs from the ordinary courtesan in that she does not let out her body on piece-work as a wage-worker, but sells it once and for all into slavery' (p. 102). It is arguable, however, that these differences have not really survived the century since Engels observed them. Certainly the vast expansion in women's education and professional employment has rendered bourgeois women financially independent in varying degrees. Certainly, too, the increase in working-class home ownership and the severe disadvantage of women workers in terms of pay and job security has made them more dependent on a male wage than Engels wanted to concede. These and other points suggest that the model put forward by Engels, differentiating sharply between proletarian and bourgeois marriage, simply does not hold true at the present time. Rosalind Delmar, in her reconsideration of *The Origin*, suggests that 'none of the distinguishing categories which Engels gives the proletarian family in capitalist conditions are discernible today'[23], and a similar conclusion might be drawn with regard to the bourgeois family.

As far as the position of women in general is concerned, many feminists have reacted critically to aspects of Engels's analysis of the situation at the time he wrote. Perhaps his greatest hostage to fortune is the comment that, with the development of female wage labour in industry, 'no basis for any kind of male supremacy is left in the proletarian household, except, perhaps, for something of the brutality toward women that has spread since the introduction of monogamy' (p. 103). The extraordinary spread of refuges for battered

23. Rosalind Delmar, 'Looking again at Engels's *Origin of the Family, Private Property and the State*' in Juliet Mitchell and Ann Oakley (eds.), *The Rights and Wrongs of Women* (Penguin, Harmondsworth, 1976), p. 283.

women, revealing the number of women previously faced with no other option than to stay with violent men, seems to give the lie to Engels's statement. (Such refuges tend to be used disproportionately by working-class women not because of greater brutality but because of fewer financial options.) In general, as many feminists have pointed out, Engels did not attend sufficiently to the amount of domestic work women have to do even when they do go out to work full time, and he certainly did not see how heavy the familial and household burden was and is on working-class women. Hence he ignored the factors that have continued to depress women's wages and keep them in part-time and insecure work, and he failed to appreciate the far-reaching effects of ideologies of what was appropriate as men's work and women's work. It must be said, however, since Engels is often misread on this point, that the one error he did *not* make was to argue that women's entry into wage work – social production outside the home – would of itself bring about women's emancipation: he thought rather that this was a first, necessary step towards emancipation. His stance is rather more radical than is often supposed, for what he actually says is that 'it will be plain that the first condition for the liberation of the wife is to bring the whole female sex back into public industry, and that this in turn demands that the characteristic of the monogamous family as the economic unit of society be abolished' (p. 105).

On all these counts – state, class marriage forms, position of women – it is difficult to see how Engels's analysis of mid to late nineteenth-century patterns can be of great relevance to us now. If we add these empirical limitations of the text to the series of anthropological and methodological criticisms discussed earlier, it might be reasonable to conclude that Engels's hastily written study has survived for too long already. Yet it remains a text that is regularly featured on course outlines and reading lists for students and frequently referred to in political debate. Although the analysis does not in my view deserve the extravagant praise that has been forthcoming from some quarters, neither does it deserve consignment to the library stacks. The reason why this work remains obdurately of interest is that the questions it deals with – often in a surprisingly spontaneous and informal way – have persisted in their importance. I want to end, therefore, with a brief discussion of why *The Origin* is such a significant text.

The Origin and Contemporary Debates

The first reason why *The Origin* is of such significance is that it has made such an important, if highly controversial, contribution not only to Marxist theory but to the policies of societies attempting to implement Marxist principles. Maxine Molyneux has argued that in the early decades of Soviet society Engels's analysis was 'codified' into a blueprint for the emancipation of women. In addition, this programme has been exported not merely to the various countries that make up the Soviet socialist bloc, but to many third-world countries that have espoused Marxist or other socialist views.[24] Hence we find a uniform acceptance that the entry of women into social production is the first step to emancipation; often, too, we find some gesture towards the 'socialization of housework', following Lenin's view that women must be got out of private immobility in the home and that this could only be done by the collectivization of these chores. These policies have tended to prove controversial where feminism is concerned, principally because they focus largely on production and fail to make significant changes to the sexual division of labour in the home, to the area of sexuality, or to the definitions of femininity and masculinity. In short, as Molyneux and other feminists have argued, they reflect at the level of policy an analysis that is excessively concerned with seeing the family in terms of property and class society, paying insufficient attention to other causes of women's oppression in the very different cultures that make up the contemporary

24. Maxine Molyneux, 'Socialist societies old and new: progress towards women's emancipation', *Feminist Review*, no. 8 (Summer 1981).

socialist world. Given the tremendous influence of this programme, however, Engels's text must necessarily be of more than academic interest: there is considerable political investment in rethinking his analysis.

Related to the question of the immense policy influence of *The Origin* is the highly controversial issue of its status as an exemplary analysis using the method of historical materialism. The work's claim to this status is based on the fact that Engels proposes a materialist explanation – not merely a description but an explanation – of how the form of the family changed as a result of changes in the mode of production. He explains the development of the monogamous family as the consequence of the amassing of private property, classically relating the explanation of a 'superstructural' phenomenon (the family) to its economic 'base'. This question of determination, of the dependence or autonomy of familial relations with regard to the economic level, underlies much that is disputed about Engels's argument. The formulation that he uses, stressing that historical materialism is concerned with the reproduction of life as well as social production, has acquired a new relevance with the development of modern socialist-feminist theory. The attempt to explore the possibility of a theoretical rapprochement between feminist theory and a Marxist analysis of capitalist society has resulted in one particular passage of Engels being cited again and again as the point of departure:

According to the materialistic conception, the determining factor in history is, in the final instance, the production and reproduction of immediate life. This, again, is of a twofold character: on the one side, the production of the means of existence, of food, clothing and shelter and the tools necessary for that production; on the other side, the production of human beings themselves, the propagation of the species. The social organization under which the people of a particular historical epoch and a particular country live is determined by both kinds of production: by the stage of development of labour on the one hand and of the family on the other (pp. 35–6).

Engels's use of the concept of reproduction – a concept on

which there now exists quite a substantial literature[25] – illustrates the way in which he tries to balance the rival claims of family and mode of production in a determinist analysis. Naturally he is criticized heavily from both sides. Many feminists argue that Engels fails to allow sufficient weight either to the family or to gender more generally, seeing the whole bundle as historically determined by changes in the form of social production. Hence the usual charge levelled against Engels from a feminist point of view is *reductionism*, and more specifically of economic reductionism, in his treatment of the family. It is argued that this economic reductionism – the attribution of the causes of family change to the mode of production – underlies Engels's failure to attend seriously to questions of sexuality, ideology, domesticity or the division of labour and power between women and men generally. Yet from within Marxism the usual critique of Engels would tend to be that he separated production from reproduction, a theoretical dualism that David McLellan calls a 'most unMarxist division between the economic and the social'.[26] Lise Vogel, in her stern categorization of *The Origin* as a 'defective text', emphasizes that Engels's counterposition of production and reproduction disturbed earlier socialist theorists with its implication that the family was an autonomous entity.[27]

Yet whatever these differences of view, it must be conceded that in one sense Engels did succeed in making a substantial contribution to a materialist analysis of gender. Rosalind Delmar concludes of *The Origin*: '. . . it asserted women's oppression as a problem of history, rather than of biology, a problem which it should be the concern of historical materialism to analyse and revolutionary politics to solve.'[28]

25. For discussion of definitional problems with the concept of reproduction, see Felicity Edholm *et al.*, 'Conceptualising women', *Critique of Anthropology*, Vol. 3, nos. 9/10 (1977); for more general discussion see Michèle Barrett, *Women's Oppression Today: Problems in Marxist Feminist Analysis* (Verso, London, 1980).

26. David McLellan, *Engels* (Fontana, London, 1977), p. 37.

27. Lise Vogel, *Marxism and the Oppression of Women: Toward a Unitary Theory* (Pluto, London, 1983), p. 91.

28. Delmar, op. cit., p. 287. (See p. 23.)

There is a third reason why current interest in *The Origin* is acute: it speaks to our renewed debates on what we understand by the term 'the family' and how this relates to an understanding of sexuality and gender in more general terms. Engels stands in a distinctive position in opposition to many banal sociological platitudes about the supposedly universal nuclear family. More negatively, few scholars of the family would now have much faith in the idea of 'laws of development' of family forms as expounded by Morgan and Engels. Recent theoretical work has tended to 'deconstruct' the imaginary unity of 'the family', challenging its status and demonstrating the historical, ethnic and class variation of kinship systems, residence arrangements, economic aspects of the household, and ideologies of family life. In this connection Rosalind Coward's recent stringent critique of Engels is quite salutary. She argues that Engels used the family as an articulating concept between classes and the state, but by accepting it as a pre-given category he was prevented from looking at precisely what the notion of 'the family' always conceals: 'The analytic priority of the family subsumed any separate consideration of the division between the sexes as an antagonistic division.'[29] Thus, according to Coward, Engels's text focuses on an imaginary unity of the family, neglecting questions that more immediately concern women's oppression. This point is in some respects contentious but it serves to highlight the problems raised by the use of the vexed and confusing term 'the family', demonstrating the need to specify more precisely whether what is at issue is sexual relations, or economic organization of households, or domestic ideology. The tendency to hypostatize 'the family' is by no means limited to Engels, and the meaning and validity of the term remain open to critical scrutiny.

Finally, it must be said that part of the charm of *The Origin* lies in the foolhardy zeal with which it tackles the question of the origin of human society. Although we all know that such attempts are doomed because unprovable, they remain

29. Rosalind Coward, *Patriarchal Precedents: Sexuality and Social Relations* (Routledge & Kegan Paul, London, 1983), p. 160.

of abiding interest. Engels has the nerve to pronounce on a question as fundamental as whether human social organization began with men in charge or with women – for this is how the issues of matrilineality and so on are always popularly constructed. However erroneous this may be in anthropological terms, it persists in being the way in which people relate to these debates about origins, and the fascination with this question cannot be denied. It is not without interest that Freud's reconstruction of the origins of human sociality is equally dubious on a methodological level, but also arouses intense interest and passion. And, since this is an argument that will run and run, perhaps it is just as well that Engels and Freud disagree with each other, leaving us plenty of room for our own speculations.

Note on the Text

The text of *The Origin of the Family, Private Property and the State* is that published by Lawrence & Wishart in 1972. It is essentially the English translation by Alick West as published in 1942, but revised against the German text as it appears in Karl Marx/Friedrich Engels, *Werke*, Vol. 21 (Dietz Verlag, Berlin, 1962), and with the spelling of names and other terms modernized.

Footnotes by Engels are indicated by the asterisk system, editorial notes by superior numbers. Unless otherwise indicated, material in square brackets within the text is of editorial origin.

Engels refers frequently to Marx's extensive summary and notes on Morgan's *Ancient Society*, now available in *The Ethnological Notebooks of Karl Marx*, transcribed and edited with an Introduction by L. Krader (Van Gorcum & Co., Assen, Netherlands, 1972). All references to Marx's writings in *The Origin*, unless otherwise indicated, are to these notes.

THE ORIGIN OF THE FAMILY, PRIVATE PROPERTY AND THE STATE

Preface to the First Edition

The following chapters are, in a sense, the execution of a bequest. No less a man than Karl Marx had made it one of his future tasks to present the results of Morgan's researches in the light of the conclusions of his own – within certain limits, I may say our – materialistic examination of history, and thus to make clear their full significance. For Morgan in his own way had discovered afresh in America the materialistic conception of history discovered by Marx forty years ago, and in his comparison of barbarism and civilization it had led him, in the main points, to the same conclusions as Marx. And just as the professional economists in Germany were for years as busy in plagiarizing *Capital* as they were persistent in attempting to kill it by silence, so Morgan's *Ancient Society*** received precisely the same treatment from the spokesmen of 'prehistoric' science in England. My work can offer only a meagre substitute for what my departed friend no longer had the time to do. But I have the critical notes which he made to his extensive extracts from Morgan, and as far as possible I reproduce them here.

According to the materialistic conception, the determining factor in history is, in the final instance, the production and reproduction of immediate life. This, again, is of a twofold

* *Ancient Society, or Researches in the Lines of Human Progress from Savagery, through Barbarism to Civilization,* by Lewis H. Morgan, London, Macmillan & Co., 1877. The book was printed in America and is peculiarly difficult to obtain in London. The author died some years ago. [For the purposes of this edition, all references to *Ancient Society* are from the World Publishing Company edition, New York, 1963.]

35

character: on the one side, the production of the means of existence, of food, clothing and shelter and the tools necessary for that production; on the other side, the production of human beings themselves, the propagation of the species. The social organization under which the people of a particular historical epoch and a particular country live is determined by both kinds of production: by the stage of development of labour on the one hand and of the family on the other. The lower the development of labour and the more limited the amount of its products, and consequently, the more limited also the wealth of the society, the more the social order is found to be dominated by kinship groups. However, within this structure of society based on kinship groups the productivity of labour increasingly develops, and with it private property and exchange, differences of wealth, the possibility of utilizing the labour power of others, and hence the basis of class antagonisms: new social elements, which in the course of generations strive to adapt the old social order to the new conditions, until at last their incompatibility brings about a complete upheaval. In the collision of the newly developed social classes, the old society founded on kinship groups is broken up. In its place appears a new society, with its control centred in the state, the subordinate units of which are no longer kinship associations, but local associations; a society in which the system of the family is completely dominated by the system of property, and in which there now freely develop those class antagonisms and class struggles that have hitherto formed the content of all *written* history.

It is Morgan's great merit that he has discovered and reconstructed in its main lines this prehistoric basis of our written history, and that in the kinship groups of the North American Indians he has found the key to the most important and hitherto insoluble riddles of earliest Greek, Roman and German history. His book is not the work of a day. For nearly 40 years he wrestled with his material until he was completely master of it. But that also makes his book one of the few epoch-making works of our time.

In the following presentation, the reader will in general

easily distinguish what comes from Morgan and what I have added. In the historical sections on Greece and Rome I have not confined myself to Morgan's evidence, but have added what was available to me. The sections on the Celts and the Germans are in the main my work; Morgan had to rely here almost entirely on secondary sources, and for German conditions – apart from Tacitus – on the worthless and liberalistic falsifications of Mr Freeman. The treatment of the economic aspects, which in Morgan's book was sufficient for his purpose but quite inadequate for mine, has been done afresh by myself. And, finally, I am, of course, responsible for all the conclusions drawn, in so far as Morgan is not expressly cited.

Friedrich Engels
1884

Preface to the Fourth Edition

The earlier large editions of this work have been out of print now for almost half a year, and for some time the publisher has been asking me to prepare a new edition. Until now, more urgent work kept me from doing so. Since the appearance of the first edition seven years have elapsed, during which our knowledge of the primitive forms of the family has made important advances. There was, therefore, plenty to do in the way of improvements and additions; all the more so as the proposed stereotyping of the present text will make any further alterations impossible for some time.

I have accordingly submitted the whole text to a careful revision and made a number of additions which, I hope, take due account of the present state of knowledge. I also give in the course of this preface a short review of the development of the history of the family from Bachofen to Morgan; I do so chiefly because the chauvinistically inclined English anthropologists are still striving their utmost to kill by silence the revolution which Morgan's discoveries have effected in our conception of primitive society, while they appropriate his results without the slightest compunction. Elsewhere also the example of England is in some cases followed only too often.

My work has been translated into a number of other languages: first, Italian – *L'origine della famiglia, della proprietà privata e dello stato, versione riveduta dall'autore, di Pasquale Martignetti*, Benevento, 1885; then, Rumanian – *Originafamiliei, proprietatei private si a statului, traducere de Joan Nadejde*, in the Jassy periodical *Contemporanul*, September 1885 to May 1886; further, Danish – *Familjens, Privatejendommens og Statens Oprin-*

delse Dansk, af Forfattern gennemgaaet Udgave, besørgen af Gerson Trier, Köbenhavn, 1888. A French translation by Henri Ravé, based on the present German edition, is on the press.

Before the beginning of the sixties, one cannot speak of a history of the family. In this field, the science of history was still completely under the influence of the Five Books of Moses. The patriarchal form of the family, which was there described in greater detail than anywhere else, was not only assumed without question to be the oldest form, but it was also identified – minus its polygamy – with the bourgeois family of today, as if the family had really experienced no historical development at all. At most it was admitted that in primitive times there might have been a period of sexual promiscuity. It is true that in addition to the monogamous form of the family, two other forms were known to exist – polygamy in the Orient and polyandry in India and Tibet; but these three forms could not be arranged in any historical order and merely appeared side by side without any connection. That among some peoples of ancient times, as well as among some savages still alive today, descent was reckoned not from the father but from the mother, and that the female line was therefore regarded as alone valid; that among many peoples of the present day in every continent marriage is forbidden within certain large groups which at that time had not been closely studied – these facts were indeed known and fresh instances of them were continually being collected. But nobody knew what to do with them, and even as late as E. B. Tylor's *Researches into the Early History of Mankind, etc.* (1865) they are listed as mere 'curious customs', side by side with the prohibition among some savages against touching burning wood with an iron tool and similar religious mumbo jumbo.

The study of the history of the family dates from 1861, from the publication of Bachofen's *Mutterrecht* [Mother Right]. In this work the author advances the following propositions: (1) That originally man lived in a state of sexual promiscuity, to describe which Bachofen uses the mistaken term 'hetaerism'; (2) that such promiscuity excludes any certainty of paternity, that descent could therefore be reckoned only in the female line, according to mother right, and that this was originally the case amongst all the peoples of antiquity; (3) that since women, as mothers, were the only parents of the younger generation that were known with certainty, they held a position of such high respect and honour that it became the foundation, in Bachofen's conception, of a regular rule of women (gyneocracy); (4) that the transition to monogamy, where the woman belonged to one man exclusively, involved a violation of a primitive religious law (that is, actually a violation of the traditional right of the other men to this woman), and that in order to expiate this violation or to purchase indulgence for it the woman had to be surrendered for a limited period.

Bachofen finds the proofs of these assertions in innumerable passages of ancient classical literature, which he collected with immense industry. According to him, the development from 'hetaerism' to monogamy and from mother right to father right is accomplished, particularly among the Greeks, as the consequence of an advance in religious conceptions, introducing into the old hierarchy of the gods, representative of the old outlook, new divinities, representative of the new outlook, who push the former more and more into the background. Thus, according to Bachofen, it is not the development of men's actual conditions of life, but the religious reflection of these conditions inside their heads, which has brought about the historical changes in the social position of the sexes in relation to each other. In accordance with this view, Bachofen interprets the *Oresteia* of Aeschylus as the dramatic representation of the conflict between declining mother right and the new father right that arose and triumphed in the heroic age. For the sake of her paramour, Aegisthus, Clytemnestra slays her husband, Agamemnon, on his return from the Trojan War; but Orestes, her son by Agamemnon avenges his father's murder by slaying his mother. For this act he is pursued by the Erinyes [Furies], the demonic guardians of mother right, according to which matricide is the gravest and most inexpiable crime. But Apollo, who by the voice of his oracle had summoned Orestes to this deed, and Athena, who is called upon to give judgement – the two deities who here represent the new patriarchal order – take Orestes under their protection; Athena hears both sides. The whole matter of the dispute is briefly summed up in the debate which now takes place between Orestes and the Erinyes. Orestes contends that Clytemnestra has committed a double crime; she has slain *her* husband and thus she has also slain *his* father. Why should the Erinyes pursue him and not her, seeing that she is by far the more guilty? The answer is striking: *'Unrelated by blood was she to the man she slew.'*

The murder of a man not related by blood, even if he be the husband of the murderess, is expiable and does not concern the Erinyes. Their office is solely to punish murder between blood relations, and of such murders the most grave and the most inexpiable, according to mother right, is matricide. Apollo now comes forward in Orestes' defence. Athena calls upon the Areopagites – the Athenian jurors – to vote. The votes for Orestes' condemnation and for his acquittal are equal. Then Athena, as President of the Court, gives her vote for Orestes and acquits him. Father right has triumphed over mother right. The 'gods of young descent', as the Erinyes themselves call them, have triumphed over the Erinyes, and the latter then finally allow themselves to be persuaded to take up a new office in the service of the new order.

This new but undoubtedly correct interpretation of the *Oresteia* is one of the best and finest passages in the whole book, but it proves at the same time that Bachofen believes at least as much as Aeschylus did in the Erinyes, Apollo and Athena; for, at bottom, he believes that the overthrow of mother right by father right was a miracle wrought during the Greek heroic age by these divinities. That such a conception, which makes religion the lever of world history, must finally end in pure mysticism, is clear. It is therefore a tough and by no means always a grateful task to plough through Bachofen's solid tome. But all that does not lessen his importance as a pioneer. He was the first to replace the vague phrases about some unknown primitive state of sexual promiscuity by proofs of the following facts: that abundant traces survive in ancient classical literature of a state prior to monogamy among the Greeks and Asiatics when not only did a man have sexual intercourse with several women, but a woman with several men, without offending against morality; that this custom did not disappear without leaving its traces in the limited surrender which was the price women had to pay for the right to monogamy; that therefore descent could originally be reckoned only in the female line, from mother to mother; that far into the period of monogamy, with its certain or at least acknowledged paternity, the female line was still alone recognized; and that the original position of the mothers, as the only certain parents of their children, secured for them, and thus for their whole sex, a higher social status than women have ever enjoyed since. Bachofen did not put these statements as clearly as this, for he was hindered by his mysticism. But he proved them; and in 1861 that was a real revolution.

Bachofen's massive volume was written in German, the language of the nation which at that time interested itself less than any other in the prehistory of the modern family. Consequently, he remained unknown. His first successor in the same field appeared in 1865, without ever having heard of Bachofen.

This successor was J. F. McLennan, the exact opposite of his predecessor. Instead of a mystic of genius, we have the dry-as-dust jurist; instead of the exuberant imagination of a poet, the plausible arguments of a barrister defending his brief. McLennan finds among many savage, barbarian, and even civilized peoples of ancient and modern times a form of marriage in which the bridegroom, alone or with his friends, must carry off the bride from her relations by a show of force. This custom must be the survival of an earlier custom when the men of one tribe did in fact carry off their wives by force from other tribes. What was the origin of this 'marriage by capture'? So long as men could find enough women in their own tribe, there was no reason whatever for it. We find, however, no less frequently that among undeveloped peoples there are certain groups (which in 1865 were still often identified with the tribes themselves) within which marriage is forbidden, so that the men are obliged to take their wives, and women their husbands, from outside the group; whereas among other peoples the custom is that the men of one group must take their wives only from within their own group. McLennan calls the first peoples 'exogamous' and the second 'endogamous'; he then promptly proceeds to construct a rigid opposition between exogamous and endogamous 'tribes'. And although his own investigations into exogamy force the fact under his nose that in many, if not in most or even in all, cases, this opposition exists only in his own imagination, he nevertheless makes it the basis of his whole theory. According to this theory, exogamous tribes can only obtain their wives from other tribes; and since in savagery there is a permanent state of war between tribe and tribe, these wives could only be obtained by capture.

McLennan then goes on to ask: whence this custom of exogamy? The conception of consanguinity and incest could not have anything to do with it, for these things only came much later. But there was another common custom among savages – the custom of killing female children immediately after birth. This would cause a surplus of men in each individual tribe, of which the inevitable and immediate consequence would be that several men possessed a wife in common (polyandry). And this would have the further consequence that it would be known who was the mother of a child, but not who its father was: hence relationship only in the female line, with exclusion of the male line – mother right. And a second consequence of the scarcity of women within a tribe – a scarcity which polyandry mitigated, but did not remove – was precisely this systematic, forcible abduction of women from other tribes.

As exogamy and polyandry are referable to one and the same cause – a want of balance between the sexes – we are forced to regard *all the exogamous races as having originally been polyandrous* ... Therefore we must hold it to be beyond dispute that among exogamous races the first system of kinship was that which recognized blood-ties through mothers only (McLennan, *Studies in Ancient History*, 1886. *Primitive Marriage*, p. 124).[1]

It is McLennan's merit to have directed attention to the general occurrence and great importance of what he calls exogamy. He did not by any means *discover* the existence of exogamous groups; still less did he understand them. Besides the early, scattered notes of many observers (these were McLennan's sources), Latham (*Descriptive Ethnology*, 1859) had given a detailed and accurate description of this institution among the Magars in India, and had said that it was very widespread and occurred in all parts of the world – a passage which McLennan himself cites. Morgan, in 1847, in his letters on the Iroquois (*American Review*) and in 1851 in *The League of the Iroquois*, had already demonstrated the existence of exogamous groups among this tribe and had given an accurate account of them; whereas McLennan, as we shall see, wrought greater confusion here with his legalistic mind than Bachofen wrought in the field of mother right with his mystical fancies. It is also a merit of McLennan that he recognized matrilineal descent as the earlier system, though he was here anticipated by Bachofen, as he later acknowledged. But McLennan is not clear on this either; he always speaks of 'kinship through females only', and this term, which is correct for an earlier stage, he continually applies to later stages of development when descent and inheritance were indeed still traced exclusively through the female line, but when kinship on the male side was also recognized and expressed. There you have the pedantic mind of the jurist, who fixes on a rigid legal term and goes on applying it unchanged when changed conditions have made it applicable no longer.

Apparently McLennan's theory, plausible though it was, did not seem any too well established even to its author. At any rate, he himself is struck by the fact that 'it is observable that the form of capture is now most distinctly marked and impressive just among those races which have *male* kinship' (should be

1. John Ferguson McLennan, *Studies in Ancient History, Comprising a Reprint of 'Primitive Marriage. An Inquiry into the Origin of the Form of Capture in Marriage Ceremonies'*, London and New York, 1886, pp. 124–5.

'descent in the male line') (ibid., p. 140). And again: 'It is a curious fact that nowhere now, that we are aware of, is infanticide *a system* where exogamy and the earliest form of kinship coexist' (ibid., p. 146). Both these facts flatly contradict his method of explanation, and he can only meet them with new and still more complicated hypotheses.

Nevertheless, his theory found great applause and support in England. McLennan was here generally regarded as the founder of the history of the family and the leading authority on the subject. However many exceptions and variations might be found in individual cases, his opposition of exogamous and endogamous tribes continued to stand as the recognized foundation of the accepted view, and to act as blinkers, obstructing any free survey of the field under investigation and so making any decisive advance impossible. Against McLennan's exaggerated reputation in England – and the English fashion is copied elsewhere – it becomes a duty to set down the fact that he has done more harm with his completely mistaken antithesis between exogamous and endogamous 'tribes' than he has done good by his research.

Facts were now already coming to light in increasing number which did not fit into his neat framework. McLennan knew only three forms of marriage: polygyny, polyandry and monogamy. But once attention had been directed to the question, more and more proofs were found that there existed among undeveloped peoples forms of marriage in which a number of men possessed a number of women in common, and Lubbock (*The Origin of Civilization*, 1870) recognized this group marriage ('communal marriage') as a historical fact.

Immediately afterwards, in 1871, Morgan came forward with new and, in many ways, decisive evidence. He had convinced himself that the peculiar system of consanguinity in force among the Iroquois was common to all the aboriginal inhabitants of the United States and therefore extended over a whole continent although it directly contradicted the degrees of relationship arising out of the system of marriage as actually practised by these peoples. He then induced the Federal government to collect information about the systems of consanguinity among the other peoples of the world and to send out for this purpose tables and lists of questions prepared by himself. He discovered from the replies: (1) that the system of consanguinity of the American Indians was also in force among numerous peoples in Asia and, in a somewhat modified form, in Africa and Australia; (2) that its complete explanation was to be found in a form of group marriage which was just dying out in Hawaii and other Australasian islands; and (3) that side by side with this form of marriage a system of consanguinity was in force in the same islands which could only be explained through a still more primitive, now extinct, form of group marriage. He published the collected evidence, together with the conclusions he drew from it, in his *Systems of Consanguinity and Affinity*, 1871, and thus carried the debate on to an infinitely wider field. By starting from the systems of consanguinity and reconstructing from them the corresponding forms of family, he opened a new line of research and extended our range of vision into the prehistory of mankind. If this method proved to be sound, McLennan's pretty theories would be completely demolished.

McLennan defended his theory in a new edition of *Primitive Marriage* (*Studies in Ancient History*, 1876). Whilst he himself constructs a highly artificial history of the family out of pure hypotheses, he demands from Lubbock and Morgan not merely proofs for every one of their statements, but proofs as indisputably valid as if they were to be submitted in evidence in a Scottish court of law. And this is the man who, from Tacitus' report on the close relationship between maternal uncle and sister's son among the Germans (*Germania*, Chap. 20), from Caesar's report that the Britons in groups of ten or twelve possessed their wives in common, and from all the other reports of classical authors on community of wives among barbarians, calmly draws the conclusion that all these peoples lived in a state of polyandry! One might be listening to a prosecuting counsel who can allow himself every liberty in arguing his own case, but demands from defending counsel the most formal, legally valid proof for his every word.

He maintains that group marriage is pure imagination, and by so doing falls far behind Bachofen. He declares that Morgan's systems of consanguinity are mere codes of conventional politeness, the proof being that the Indians also address a stranger or a white man as 'brother' or 'father'. One might as well say that the terms 'father', 'mother', 'brother', and 'sister' are mere meaningless forms of address because Catholic priests and abbesses are addressed as 'father' and 'mother', and because monks and nuns, and even freemasons and members of English trade unions and associations at their full sessions, are addressed as 'brother' and 'sister'. In a word, McLennan's defence was miserably feeble.

But on one point he had still not been assailed. The opposition of exogamous and endogamous 'tribes' on which his whole system rested not only remained unshaken, but was even universally acknowledged as the keystone of the whole history of the family. McLennan's attempt to explain this opposition might be inadequate and in contradiction with his own facts. But the antithesis itself, the existence of two mutually exclusive types of self-sufficient and independent tribes, of which the one type took their wives from within the tribe, while the other type absolutely forbade it – that was sacred gospel. Compare, for example, Giraud-Teulon's *Origines de la famille* (1874) and even Lubbock's *Origin of Civilization* (fourth edition, 1882).

Here Morgan takes the field with his main work, *Ancient Society* (1877), the work that underlies the present study. What Morgan had only dimly guessed in 1871 is now developed in full consciousness. There is no antithesis between endogamy and exogamy; up to the present, the existence of exogamous 'tribes' has not been demonstrated anywhere. But at the time when group marriage still prevailed – and in all probability it prevailed everywhere at some time – the tribe was subdivided into a number of groups related by blood on the mother's side, gentes, within which it was strictly forbidden to marry, so that the men of a gens, though they could take their wives from within the tribe and generally did so, were compelled to take them from outside their gens. Thus while each gens was strictly exogamous, the tribe embracing all the gentes was no less endogamous – which finally disposed of the last remains of McLennan's artificial constructions.

But Morgan did not rest here. Through the gens of the American Indians, he was enabled to make his second great advance in his field of research. In this gens, organized according to mother right, he discovered the primitive form out of which had developed the later gens organized according to father right, the gens as we find it among the ancient civilized peoples. The Greek and Roman gens, the old riddle of all historians, now found its explanation in the Indian gens, and a new foundation was thus laid for the whole of primitive history.

This rediscovery of the primitive matriarchal gens as the earlier stage of the patriarchal gens of civilized peoples has the same importance for anthropology as Darwin's theory of evolution has for biology and Marx's theory of surplus value for political economy. It enabled Morgan to outline for the first time a history of the family in which for the present, so far as the material now available permits, at least the classic stages of development in their main outlines are now determined. That this opens a new epoch in the treatment of primitive history must be clear to everyone. The matriarchal gens has become the pivot on which the whole science turns; since its discovery we know where to look and what to look for in our research, and how to arrange the results. And, consequently, since Morgan's book, progress in this field has been made at a far more rapid speed.

Anthropologists, even in England, now generally appreciate, or rather appropriate, Morgan's discoveries. But hardly one of them has the honesty to admit that it is to Morgan that we owe this revolution in our ideas. In England they try to kill his book by silence, and dispose of its author with condescending praise for his *earlier* achievements; they niggle endlessly over details and remain obstinately silent about his really great discoveries. The original edition of *Ancient Society* is out of print; in America there is no sale for such things; in

England, it seems, the book was systematically suppressed, and the only edition of this epoch-making work still circulating in the book trade is – the German translation.

Why this reserve? It is difficult not to see in it a conspiracy of silence; for politeness' sake, our recognized anthropologists generally pack their writings with quotations and other tokens of camaraderie. Is it, perhaps, because Morgan is an American, and for the English anthropologists it goes sorely against the grain that, despite their highly creditable industry in collecting material, they should be dependent for their general points of view in the arrangement and grouping of this material, for their ideas in fact, on two foreigners of genius, Bachofen and Morgan? They might put up with the German – but the American? Every Englishman turns patriotic when he comes up against an American, and of this I saw highly entertaining instances in the United States. Moreover, McLennan was, so to speak, the officially appointed founder and leader of the English school of anthropology. It was almost a principle of anthropological etiquette to speak of his artificially constructed historical series – child murder, polygyny, marriage by capture, matriarchal family – in tones only of profoundest respect. The slightest doubt in the existence of exogamous and endogamous 'tribes' of absolute mutual exclusiveness was considered rank heresy. Morgan had committed a kind of sacrilege in dissolving all these hallowed dogmas into thin air. Into the bargain, he had done it in such a way that it only needed saying to carry immediate conviction; so that the McLennanites, who had hitherto been helplessly reeling to and fro between exogamy and endogamy, could only beat their brows and exclaim: 'How could we be such fools as not to think of that for ourselves long ago?'

As if these crimes had not already left the official school with the option only of coldly ignoring him, Morgan filled the measure to overflowing by not merely criticizing civilization, the society of commodity production, the basic form of present-day society, in a manner reminiscent of Fourier, but also by speaking of a future transformation of this society in words which Karl Marx might have used. He had therefore amply merited McLennan's indignant reproach that 'the historical method is antipathetical to Mr Morgan's mind', and its echo as late as 1884 from Professor Giraud-Teulon of Geneva. In (1874) *Origines de la famille* this same gentleman was still groping helplessly in the maze of the McLennanite exogamy, from which Morgan had to come and rescue him!

Of the other advances which primitive anthropology owes to Morgan, I do not need to speak here; they are sufficiently discussed in the course of this study. The 14 years which have elapsed since the publication of his chief work have greatly enriched the material available for the study of the history of primitive human societies. The anthropologists, travellers and primitive historians by profession have now been joined by the comparative jurists, who have contributed either new material or new points of view. As a result, some of Morgan's minor hypotheses have been shaken or even disproved. But not one of the great leading ideas of his work has been ousted by this new material. The order which he introduced into primitive history still holds in its main lines today. It is, in fact, winning recognition to the same degree in which Morgan's responsibility for the great advance is carefully concealed.*

Friedrich Engels
London, June 16, 1891

* On the voyage back from New York in September 1888, I met a former member of Congress for the district of Rochester, who had known Lewis Morgan. Unfortunately, he could not tell me very much about him. He said that Morgan had lived in Rochester as a private individual, occupied only with his studies. His brother was a colonel, and had held a post in the War Department in Washington; it was through him that Morgan had managed to interest the government in his researches and to get several of his works published at public expense. While he was a member of Congress, my informant had also on more than one occasion used his influence on Morgan's behalf.

CHAPTER I

Stages of Prehistoric Culture

Morgan was the first person with expert knowledge to attempt to introduce a definite order into the history of primitive man; so long as no important additional material makes changes necessary, his classification will undoubtedly remain in force.

Of the three main epochs – savagery, barbarism, and civilization – he is concerned, of course, only with the first two and the transition to the third. He divides both savagery and barbarism into lower, middle, and upper stages according to the progress made in the production of food; for, he says:

> Upon their skill in this direction, the whole question of human supremacy on the earth depended. Mankind are the only beings who may be said to have gained an absolute control [Engels inserts 'almost'] over the production of food . . . It is accordingly probable that the great epochs of human progress have been identified, more or less directly, with the enlargement of the sources of subsistence [p. 19].

The development of the family takes a parallel course, but here the periods have not such striking marks of differentiation.

1. Savagery

(a) *Lower stage*. Childhood of the human race. Man still lived in his original habitat, in tropical or subtropical forests, and was partially at least a tree-dweller, for otherwise his survival among huge beasts of prey cannot be explained. Fruit, nuts and roots served him for food. The development of articulate speech is the main result of this period. Of all the peoples known to history none was still at this primitive level. Though this period may have lasted thousands of years we have no direct evidence to prove its existence; but once the evolution of man from the animal kingdom is admitted, such a transitional stage must necessarily be assumed.

(b) *Middle stage*. Begins with the utilization of fish for food (including crabs, mussels, and other aquatic animals) and with the use of fire. The two are complementary, since fish becomes fully available only by the use of fire. With this new source of nourishment, men now became independent of climate and locality; even as savages, they could, by following the rivers and coasts, spread over most of the earth. Proof of these migrations is the distribution over every continent of the crudely worked, unpolished flint tools of the earlier Stone Age, known as 'paleoliths', all or most of which date from this period. New environments, ceaseless exercise of this inventive faculty, and the ability to produce fire by friction led man to discover new kinds of food: farinaceous roots and tubers, for instance, were baked in hot ashes or in ground ovens. With the invention of the first weapons, club and spear, game could sometimes be added to the fare. But the tribes which figure in books as living entirely, that is, exclusively, by hunting never existed in reality; the yield of the hunt was far too precarious. At this stage, owing to the continual uncertainty of food supplies, cannibalism seems to have arisen and was practised from now onwards for a long time. The Australian aborigines and many of the Polynesians are still in this middle stage of savagery today.

(c) *Upper stage*. Begins with the invention of the bow and arrow, whereby game became a regular source of food, and hunting a normal form of work. Bow, string, and arrow already constitute a very complex instrument, whose invention implies long, accumulated experience and sharpened intelligence and therefore knowledge of many other inventions as well. We find, in fact, that the peoples acquainted with the bow and arrow but not yet with pottery (from which Morgan dates the transition to barbarism) are already making some beginnings towards settlement in villages and have gained some control over the production of means of subsistence; we find wooden vessels and utensils; finger-weaving (without looms) with filaments of bark; plaited baskets of bast or osier; sharpened (neolithic) stone tools. With the discovery of fire and the stone axe, dugout canoes now become common; beams and planks are also sometimes used for building houses. We find all these advances, for instance, among the Indians of north-west America, who are acquainted with the bow and arrow but not with pottery. The bow and arrow was for savagery what the iron sword was for barbarism and firearms for civilization – the decisive weapon.

2. Barbarism

(a) *Lower stage.* Dates from the introduction of pottery. In many cases it has been proved, and in all it is probable, that the first pots originated from the habit of covering baskets or wooden vessels with clay to make them fireproof; in this way it was soon discovered that the clay mould answered the purpose without any inner vessel.

Thus far we have been able to follow a general line of development applicable to all peoples at a given period without distinction of place. With the beginning of barbarism, however, we have reached a stage when the difference in the natural endowments of the two hemispheres of the earth comes into play. The characteristic feature of the period of barbarism is the domestication and breeding of animals and the cultivation of plants. Now, the Eastern Hemisphere, the so-called Old World, possessed nearly all the animals adaptable to domestication, and all the varieties of cultivable cereals except one; the Western Hemisphere, America, had no mammals that could be domesticated except the llama, which, moreover, was only found in one part of South America, and of all the cultivable cereals only one, though that was the best, namely, maize. Owing to these differences in natural conditions, the population of each hemisphere now goes on its way, and different landmarks divide the particular stages in each of the two cases.

(b) *Middle stage.* Begins in the Eastern Hemisphere with domestication of animals; in the Western, with the cultivation, by means of irrigation, of plants for food, and with the use of adobe (sun-dried) bricks and stone for building.

We will begin with the Western Hemisphere, as here this stage was never superseded before the European conquest.

At the time when they were discovered, the Indians at the lower stage of barbarism (comprising all the tribes living east of the Mississippi) were already practising some horticulture of maize and possibly also of pumpkins, melons, and other garden plants, from which they obtained a very considerable part of their food. They lived in wooden houses in villages protected by stockades. The tribes in the north-west, particularly those in the region of the Columbia River, were still at the upper stage of savagery and acquainted neither with pottery nor with any form of horticulture. The so-called Pueblo Indians of New Mexico, however, and the Mexicans, Central Americans, and Peruvians at the time of the Conquest were at the middle stage of barbarism. They lived in houses like fortresses, made of adobe brick or of stone, and cultivated maize and other plants, varying according to locality and climate, in artificially irrigated plots of ground, which supplied their main source of food; some animals even had also been domesticated – the turkey and other birds by the Mexicans, the llama by the Peruvians. They could also work metals, but not iron; hence they were still unable to dispense with stone weapons and tools. The Spanish Conquest then cut short any further independent development.

In the Eastern Hemisphere the middle stage of barbarism began with the domestication of animals providing milk and meat, but horticulture seems to have remained unknown far into this period. It was, apparently, the domestication and breeding of animals and the formation of herds of considerable size that led to the differentiation of the Aryans and

Semites from the mass of barbarians. The European and Asiatic Aryans still have the same names for cattle, but those for most of the cultivated plants are already different.

In suitable localities, the keeping of herds led to a pastoral life; the Semites lived upon the grassy plains of the Euphrates and Tigris, and the Aryans upon those of India, of the Oxus and Jaxartes, and of the Don and the Dnieper. It must have been on the borders of such pasture lands that animals were first domesticated. To later generations, consequently, the pastoral tribes appear to have come from regions which, so far from being the cradle of mankind, were almost uninhabitable for their savage ancestors and even for man at the lower stages of barbarism. But having once accustomed themselves to pastoral life in the grassy plains of the rivers, these barbarians of the middle period would never have dreamed of returning willingly to the native forests of their ancestors. Even when they were forced further to the north and west, the Semites and Aryans could not move into the forest regions of western Asia and of Europe until by cultivation of grain they had made it possible to pasture and especially to winter their herds on this less favourable land. It is more than probable that among these tribes the cultivation of grain originated from the need for cattle fodder and only later became important as a human food supply.

The plentiful supply of milk and meat and especially the beneficial effect of these foods on the growth of the children account perhaps for the superior development of the Aryan and Semitic races. It is a fact that the Pueblo Indians of New Mexico, who are reduced to an almost entirely vegetarian diet, have a smaller brain than the Indians at the lower stage of barbarism, who eat more meat and fish. In any case, cannibalism now gradually dies out, surviving only as a religious act or as a means of working magic, which is here almost the same thing.

(c) *Upper stage.* Begins with the smelting of iron ore and passes into civilization with the invention of alphabetic writing and its use for literary records. This stage (as we have seen, only the Eastern Hemisphere passed through it independently) is richer in advances in production than all the preceding stages together. To it belong the Greeks of the heroic age, the tribes of Italy shortly before the foundation of Rome, the Germans of Tacitus and the Norsemen of the Viking age.

Above all, we now first meet the iron ploughshare drawn by cattle, which made large-scale agriculture, the cultivation of fields, possible and thus created a practically unrestricted food supply in comparison with previous conditions. This led to the clearance of forest land for tillage and pasture, which in turn was impossible on a large scale without the iron axe and the iron spade. Population rapidly increased in number, and in small areas became dense. Prior to field agriculture, conditions must have been very exceptional if they allowed half a million people to be united under a central organization; probably such a thing never occurred.

We find the upper stage of barbarism at its highest in the Homeric poems, particularly in the *Iliad*. Fully developed iron tools, the bellows, the hand mill, the potter's wheel, the making of oil and wine, metal work developing almost into a fine art, the wagon and the war chariot, shipbuilding with beams and planks, the beginnings of architecture as art, walled cities with towers and battlements, the Homeric epic and a complete mythology – these are the chief legacy brought by the Greeks from barbarism into civilization. When we compare the descriptions which Caesar and even Tacitus give of the Germans, who stood at the beginning of the cultural stage from which the Homeric Greeks were just preparing to make the next advance, we realize how rich was the development of production within the upper stage of barbarism.

The sketch which I have given here, following Morgan, of the development of mankind through savagery and barbarism to the beginnings of civilization, is already rich enough in new features; what is more, they cannot be disputed since they are drawn directly from the process of production. Yet my sketch will seem flat and feeble compared with the picture to be unrolled at the end of our travels; only then will the transition from barbarism to civilization stand out in full light and in all its striking contrasts. For the time being, Morgan's division may be summarized thus: Savagery – the period in which man's appropriation of products in their natural state predominates; the products of human art are chiefly instruments which assist this appropriation. Barbarism – the period during which man learns to breed domestic animals and to practise agriculture, and acquires methods of increasing the supply of natural products by human activity. Civilization – the period in which man learns a more advanced application of work to the products of nature, the period of industry proper and of art.

CHAPTER II

The Family

Morgan, who spent a great part of his life among the Iroquois Indians – settled to this day in New York State – and was adopted into one of their tribes (the Senecas), found in use among them a system of consanguinity which was in contradiction to their actual family relationships. There prevailed among them a form of monogamy easily terminable on both sides, which Morgan calls the 'pairing family'. The issue of the married pair was therefore known and recognized by everybody: there could be no doubt about whom to call father, mother, son, daughter, brother, sister. But these names were actually used quite differently. The Iroquois calls not only his own children his sons and daughters, but also the children of his brothers; and they call him father. The children of his sisters, however, he calls his nephews and nieces, and they call him their uncle. The Iroquois woman, on the other hand, calls her sisters' children, as well as her own, her sons and daughters, and they call her mother. But her brothers' children she calls her nephews and nieces, and she is known as their aunt. Similarly, the children of brothers call one another brother and sister, and so do the children of sisters. A woman's own children and the children of her brother, on the other hand, call one another cousins. And these are not mere empty names, but expressions of actual conceptions of nearness and remoteness, of equality and difference in the degrees of consanguinity: these conceptions serve as the foundation of a fully elaborated system of consanguinity through which several hundred different relationships of one individual can be expressed. What is more, this system is not

58

only in full force among all American Indians (no exception has been found up to the present), but also retains its validity almost unchanged among the aborigines of India, the Dravidian tribes in the Deccan and the Gaura tribes in Hindustan. To this day the Tamils of southern India and the Iroquois Seneca Indians in New York State still express more than two hundred degrees of consanguinity in the same manner. And among these tribes of India, as among all the American Indians, the actual relationships arising out of the existing form of the family contradict the system of consanguinity.

How is this to be explained? In view of the decisive part played by consanguinity in the social structure of all savage and barbarian peoples, the importance of a system so widespread cannot be dismissed with phrases. When a system is general throughout America and also exists in Asia among peoples of a quite different race, when numerous instances of it are found with greater or less variation in every part of Africa and Australia, then that system has to be historically explained, not talked out of existence, as McLennan, for example, tried to do. The names of father, child, brother and sister are no mere complimentary forms of address; they involve quite definite and very serious mutual obligations which together make up an essential part of the social constitution of the peoples in question.

The explanation was found. In the Sandwich Islands (Hawaii) there still existed in the first half of the nineteenth century a form of family in which the fathers and mothers, brothers and sisters, sons and daughters, uncles and aunts, nephews and nieces were exactly what is required by the American and ancient Indian system of consanguinity. But now comes a strange thing. Once again, the system of consanguinity in force in Hawaii did not correspond to the actual form of the Hawaiian family. For according to the Hawaiian system of consanguinity all children of brothers and sisters are without exception brothers and sisters of one another and are considered to be the common children not only of their mother and her sisters or of their father and his brothers, but of all the brothers and sisters of both their parents without distinction. While, therefore, the American system of consanguinity presupposes a more primitive form of the family which has disappeared in America, but still actually exists in Hawaii, the Hawaiian system of consanguinity, on the other hand, points to a still earlier form of the family which, though we can nowhere prove it to be still in existence, nevertheless *must* have existed; for otherwise the corresponding system of consanguinity could never have arisen.

The family [says Morgan] represents an active principle. It is never stationary, but advances from a lower to a higher form as society advances from a lower to a higher condition . . . Systems of consanguinity, on the contrary, are passive; recording the progress made by the family at long intervals apart, and only changing radically when the family has radically changed [p. 444].

'And,' adds Marx, 'the same is true of the political, juridical, religious, and philosophical systems in general.' While the family undergoes living changes, the system of consanguinity ossifies; while the system survives by force of custom, the family outgrows it. But just as Cuvier could deduce from the marsupial bone of an animal skeleton found near Paris that it belonged to a marsupial animal and that extinct marsupial animals once lived there, so with the same certainty we can deduce from the historical survival of a system of consanguinity that an extinct form of family once existed which corresponded to it.

The systems of consanguinity and the forms of the family we have just mentioned differ from those of today in the fact that every child has more than one father and mother. In the American system of consanguinity, to which the Hawaiian family corresponds, brother and sister cannot be the father and mother of the same child; but the Hawaiian system of consanguinity, on the contrary, presupposes a family in which this was the rule. Here we find ourselves among forms of family which directly contradict those hitherto generally assumed to be alone valid. The traditional view recognizes only monogamy, with, in addition, polygamy on the part of individual men, and at the very most polyandry on the part of individual women; being the view of moralizing philistines, it conceals the fact that in practice these barriers raised by official society are quietly and calmly ignored. The study of primitive history, however, reveals conditions where the men live in polygamy and their wives in polyandry at the same time, and their common children are therefore considered common to them all – and these conditions in their turn undergo a long series of changes before they finally end in monogamy. The trend of these changes is to narrow more and more the circle of people comprised within the common bond of marriage, which was originally very wide, until at last it includes only the single pair, the dominant form of marriage today.

Reconstructing thus the past history of the family, Morgan, in agreement with most of his colleagues, arrives at a primitive stage when unrestricted sexual freedom prevailed within the tribe, every woman belonging equally to every man and every man to every woman. Since the eighteenth century there had been talk of such a primitive state, but only in general phrases. Bachofen – and this is one of his great merits – was the first to take the existence of such a state seriously and to search for its traces in historical and religious survivals. Today we know that the traces he found do not lead back to a social stage of promiscuous sexual intercourse, but to a much later form – namely, group marriage. The primitive social stage of promiscuity, if it ever existed, belongs to such a remote epoch that we can hardly expect to prove its existence *directly* by discovering its social fossils among backward savages. Bachofen's merit consists in having brought this question to the forefront for examination.*

Lately it has become fashionable to deny the existence of

* Bachofen proves how little he understood his own discovery, or rather his guess, by using the term 'hetaerism' to describe this primitive state. For the Greeks, when they introduced the word, hetaerism meant intercourse of men, unmarried or living in monogamy, with unmarried women; it always presupposes a definite form of marriage outside which this intercourse takes place and includes at least the possibility of prostitution. The word was this initial stage in human sexual life. Humanity must be spared this 'shame'. It is pointed out that all direct proof of such a stage is lacking, and particular appeal is made to the evidence from the rest of the animal world; for, even among animals, according to the numerous facts collected by Letourneau (*Evolution du mariage et de la famille*, 1888), complete promiscuity in sexual intercourse marks a low stage of development. But the only conclusion I can draw from all these facts, so far as man and his primitive conditions of life are concerned, is that they prove nothing whatever. That vertebrates mate together for a considerable period is sufficiently explained by physiological causes – in the case of birds, for example, by the female's need for help during the brooding period; examples of faithful monogamy among birds prove nothing about man for the simple reason that men are not descended from birds. And if strict monogamy is the height of all virtue, then the palm must go to the tapeworm, which has a complete set of male and female sexual organs in each of its 50 to 200 proglottides or sections, and spends its whole life copulating in all its sections with itself. Confining ourselves to mammals, however, we find all forms of sexual life – promiscuity, indications of group marriage, polygyny, monogamy. Polyandry alone is lacking – it took human beings to achieve that. Even our nearest relations, the quadrumana, exhibit every possible variation in the grouping of males and females; and if we narrow it down still more and consider only the four anthropoid apes, all that Letourneau has to say about them is that they are sometimes monogamous, sometimes polygamous, while Saussure, quoted by Giraud-Teulon, maintains that they are monogamous. The more recent assertions of the monogamous habits of the anthropoid apes which are cited by Westermarck

---

never used in any other sense, and it is in this sense that I use it with Morgan. Bachofen everywhere introduces into his extremely important discoveries the most incredible mystifications through his notion that in their historical development the relations between men and women had their origin in men's contemporary religious conceptions, not in their actual conditions of life.

(*The History of Human Marriage*, London, 1891) are also very far from proving anything. In short, our evidence is such that honest Letourneau admits: 'Among mammals there is no strict relation between the degree of intellectual development and the form of sexual life.' And Espinas (*Des sociétés animales*, 1877) says in so many words:

> The herd is the highest social group which we can observe among animals. It is composed, *so it appears*, of families, but from the start *the family and the herd are in conflict with one another* and develop in inverse proportion.

As the above shows, we know practically nothing definite about the family and other social groupings of the anthropoid apes; the evidence is flatly contradictory, which is not to be wondered at. The evidence with regard to savage human tribes is contradictory enough, requiring very critical examination and sifting, and ape societies are far more difficult to observe than human. For the present, therefore, we must reject any conclusion drawn from such completely unreliable reports.

The sentence quoted from Espinas, however, provides a better starting point. Among the higher animals the herd and the family are not complementary to one another, but antagonistic. Espinas shows very well how the jealousy of the males during the mating season loosens the ties of every social herd or temporarily breaks it up.

> When the family bond is close and exclusive, herds form only in exceptional cases. When on the other hand free sexual intercourse or polygamy prevails, the herd comes into being almost spontaneously . . . Before a herd can be formed, family ties must be loosened and the individual must have become free again. This is the reason why organized flocks are so rarely found among birds . . . We find more or less organized societies among mammals, however, precisely because here the individual is not merged in the family . . . In its first growth, therefore, the common feeling of the herd has no greater enemy than the common feeling of the family. We state it without hesitation: only by absorbing families which had undergone a radical change could a social form higher than the family have developed; at the same time, these families were thereby enabled

later to constitute themselves afresh under infinitely more favourable circumstances [Espinas, op. cit., quoted by Giraud-Teulon, *Origines du mariage et de la famille*, 1884, pp. 518–20].

Here we see that animal societies are, after all, of some value for drawing conclusions about human societies; but the value is only negative. So far as our evidence goes, the higher vertebrates know only two forms of family – polygyny or separate couples; each form allows only *one* adult male, only one husband. The jealousy of the male, which both consolidates and isolates the family, sets the animal family in opposition to the herd. The jealousy of the males prevents the herd, the higher social form, from coming into existence, or weakens its cohesion, or breaks it up during the mating period; at best, it attests to its development. This alone is sufficient proof that animal families and primitive human society are incompatible, and that when primitive men were working their way up from the animal creation, they either had no family at all or a form that does not occur among animals. In small numbers, an animal so defenceless as evolving man might struggle along even in conditions of isolation, with no higher social grouping than the single male and female pair, such as Westermarck, following the reports of hunters, attributes to the gorillas and the chimpanzees. For man's development beyond the level of the animals, for the achievement of the greatest advance nature can show, something more was needed: the power of defence lacking to the individual had to be made good by the united strength and cooperation of the herd. To explain the transition to humanity from conditions such as those in which the anthropoid apes live today would be quite impossible; it looks much more as if these apes had strayed off the line of evolution and were gradually dying out or at least degenerating. That alone is sufficient ground for rejecting all attempts based on parallels drawn between their forms of family and those of primitive man. Mutual toleration among the adult males, freedom from jealousy, was the first condition for the formation of those larger, permanent groups in which alone animals could become men. And what, in fact, do we find to be the oldest and most primitive form of family whose historical existence we can indisputably prove and which in one or two parts of the world we can still study today? – group marriage, the form of family in which whole groups of men and whole groups of women mutually possess one another, and which leaves little room for jealousy. And at a later stage of development we find the exceptional form of polyandry, which positively revolts every jealous instinct and is therefore unknown among animals. But, as all known forms of group marriage are accompanied by such peculiarly complicated regulations that they necessarily point to earlier and simpler forms of sexual relations, and therefore in the last resort to a period of promiscuous intercourse corresponding to the transition from the animal to the human, the references to animal marriages only bring us back to the very point from which we were to be led away for good and all.

What, then, does promiscuous sexual intercourse really mean? It means the absence of prohibitions and restrictions which are or have been in force. We have already seen the barrier of jealousy go down. If there is one thing certain, it is that the feeling of jealousy develops relatively late. The same is true of the conception of incest. Not only were brother and sister originally man and wife, sexual intercourse between parents and children is still permitted among many peoples today. Bancroft (*The Native Races of the Pacific States of North America*, 1875, Vol. I), testifies to it among the Kaviats on the Bering Straits, the Kadiaks near Alaska, and the Tinneh in the interior of British North America. Letourneau compiled reports of it among the Chippewa Indians, the Cucus in Chile, the Caribs, the Karens in Burma – to say nothing of the stories told by the old Greeks and Romans about the Parthians, Persians, Scythians, Huns, and so on. Before incest was invented – for incest *is* an invention, and a very valuable one, too – sexual intercourse between parents and children did not arouse any more repulsion than sexual intercourse between other persons of different generations, and that occurs today even in the most philistine countries without exciting any great horror; even 'old maids' of over 60, if they are rich enough, sometimes marry young men in their 30s. But if we consider the most primitive known forms of family apart from their conceptions of incest – conceptions which are totally different from ours and frequently in direct contradiction to them – then the form of sexual intercourse can only be described as promiscuous – promiscuous in so far as the restrictions later established by custom did not yet exist. But in everyday practice that by no means necessarily implies general mixed mating. Temporary pairings of one man with one woman were not in any way excluded, just as in the cases of group marriages today the majority of relationships are of this character. And when Westermarck, the latest writer to deny the existence of such a primitive state, applies the term 'marriage' to every relationship in which the two sexes remain mated until the birth of the offspring, we must point out that this kind of marriage can very well occur under the conditions of promiscuous intercourse without contradicting the principle of promiscuity – the absence of any restriction imposed by custom on sexual intercourse. Westermarck, however, takes the standpoint that promiscuity 'involves a suppression of individual inclinations', and that therefore 'the most genuine form of it is prostitution'. In my opinion, any understanding of primitive society is impossible to people who only see it as a brothel. We will return to this point when discussing group marriage.

According to Morgan, from this primitive state of promiscuous intercourse there developed, probably very early:

1. The Consanguine Family, the First Stage of the Family

Here the marriage groups are separated according to generations: all the grandfathers and grandmothers within the limits of the family are all husbands and wives of one another; so are also their children, the fathers and mothers; the latter's children will form a third circle of common husbands and wives; and their children, the great-grandchildren of the first group, will form a fourth. In this form of marriage, therefore, only ancestors and progeny, and parents and children, are excluded from the rights and duties (as we should say) of marriage with one another. Brothers and sisters, male and female cousins of the first, second, and more remote degrees, are all brothers and sisters of one another, and *precisely for that reason* they are all husbands and wives of one another. At this stage the relationship of brother and sister also includes as a matter of course the practice of sexual intercourse with one another.* In its typical form, such a family would consist of the descendants of a single pair, the descendants of these descendants in each generation being again brothers and sisters, and therefore husbands and wives, of one another.

* In a letter written in the spring of 1882, Marx expresses himself in the strongest terms about the complete misrepresentation of primitive times in Wagner's text to the *Nibelungen:* 'Have such things been heard, that brother embraced sister as a bride?' To Wagner and his 'lecherous gods' who, quite in the modern manner, spice their love affairs with a little incest, Marx replies: 'In primitive times the sister *was* the wife, *and that was moral.'*

[*To the Fourth edition.*] A French friend of mine [Bonnier] who is an admirer of Wagner is not in agreement with this note. He observes that already in the Elder Edda, on which Wagner based his story, in the *Oegisdrecka*, Loki makes the reproach to Freya: 'In the sight of the gods thou didst embrace thine own brother.' Marriage between brother and sister, he argues, was therefore forbidden already at that time. The *Oegisdrecka* is the expression of a time when belief in the old myths had completely broken down; it is purely a satire on the gods, in the style of Lucian. If Loki as Mephistopheles makes such a reproach to Freya, it tells rather against Wagner. Loki also says some lines later to Njord: 'With thy sister didst thou breed such a son' (*vidh systur thinni gaztu slikan mög*). Njord is not, indeed, an Asa, but a Vana, and says in the Ynglinga saga that marriages between brothers and sisters are usual in Vanaland, which was not the case among the Asas. This would seem to show that the Vanas were more ancient gods than the Asas. At any rate, Njord lives among the Asas as one of themselves, and therefore the *Oegisdrecka* is rather a proof that at the time when the Norse sagas of the gods arose, marriages between brothers and sisters, at any rate among the gods, did not yet excite any horror. If one wants to find excuses for Wagner, it would perhaps be better to cite Goethe instead of the Edda, for in his ballad of the God and the Bayadere Goethe commits a similar mistake in regard to the religious surrender of women, which he makes far too similar to modern prostitution.

The consanguine family is extinct. Even the most primitive peoples known to history provide no demonstrable instance of it. But that it *must* have existed, we are compelled to admit; for the Hawaiian system of consanguinity still prevalent today throughout the whole of Polynesia expresses degrees of consanguinity which could only arise in this form of family; and the whole subsequent development of the family presupposes the existence of the consanguine family as a necessary preparatory stage.

2. *The Punaluan Family*

If the first advance in organization consisted in the exclusion of parents and children from sexual intercourse with one another, the second was the exclusion of sister and brother. On account of the greater nearness in age, this second advance was infinitely more important, but also more difficult, than the first. It was effected gradually, beginning probably with the exclusion from sexual intercourse of one's own brothers and sisters (children of the same mother) first in isolated cases and then by degrees as a general rule (even in this century exceptions were found in Hawaii), and ending with the prohibition of marriage even between collateral brothers and sisters, or, as we should say, between first, second, and third cousins. It affords, says Morgan, 'a good illustration of the operation of the principle of natural selection'. There can be no question that the tribes among whom inbreeding was restricted by this advance were bound to develop more quickly and more fully than those among whom marriage between brothers and sisters remained the rule and the law. How powerfully the influence of this advance made itself felt is seen in the institution which arose directly out of it and went far beyond it – the gens, which forms the basis of the social order of most, if not all, barbarian peoples of the earth and from which in Greece and Rome we step directly into civilization.

After a few generations at most, every original family was

bound to split up. The practice of living together in a primitive communistic household which prevailed without exception till late in the middle stage of barbarism set a limit, varying with the conditions but fairly definite in each locality, to the maximum size of the family community. As soon as the conception arose that sexual intercourse between children of the same mother was wrong, it was bound to exert its influence when the old households split up and new ones were founded (though these did not necessarily coincide with the family group). One or more lines of sisters would form the nucleus of the one household and their own brothers the nucleus of the other. It must have been in some such manner as this that the form which Morgan calls the punaluan family originated out of the consanguine family. According to the Hawaiian custom, a number of sisters, natural or collateral (first, second or more remote cousins) were the common wives of their common husbands, from among whom, however, their own brothers were excluded. These husbands now no longer called themselves brothers, for they were no longer necessarily brothers, but *punalua* – that is, intimate companion, or partner. Similarly, a line of natural or collateral brothers had a number of women, *not* their sisters, as common wives, and these wives called one another *punalua*. This was the classic form of family structure [*Familienformation*], in which later a number of variations was possible, but whose essential feature was the mutually common possession of husbands and wives within a definite family circle, from which, however, the brothers of the wives – first one's own and later also collateral – and conversely also the sisters of the husbands, were excluded.

This form of the family provides with the most complete exactness the degrees of consanguinity expressed in the American system. The children of my mother's sisters are still her children, just as the children of my father's brothers are also his children; and they are all my brothers and sisters. But the children of my mother's brothers are now her nephews and nieces, the children of my father's sisters are his nephews and nieces, and they are all my cousins. For while the husbands of my mother's sisters are still her husbands, and the wives of my father's brothers are still his wives (in right, if not always in fact), the social ban on sexual intercourse between brothers and sisters has now divided the children of brothers and sisters, who had hitherto been treated as one's own brothers and sisters, into two classes. Those in the one class remain brothers and sisters as before (collateral, according to our system). Those in the other class, the children of my mother's brother in the one case and of my father's sister in the other, *cannot* be brothers and sisters any longer; they can no longer have common parents, neither father nor mother nor both, and therefore now for the first time the class of nephews and nieces, male and female cousins, becomes necessary, which in the earlier composition of the family would have been senseless. The American system of consanguinity, which appears purely nonsensical in any form of family based on any variety of monogamy, finds, down to the smallest details, its rational explanation and its natural foundation in the punaluan family. The punaluan family or a form similar to it must have been at the very least as widespread as this system of consanguinity.

Evidence of this form of family, whose existence has actually been proved in Hawaii, would probably have been received from all over Polynesia if the pious missionaries, like the Spanish monks of former days in America, had been able to see in such unchristian conditions anything more than a sheer 'abomination'.* Caesar's report of the Britons, who were at that time in the middle stage of barbarism, 'every ten or twelve have wives in common, especially brothers with brothers and parents with children', is best explained as group marriage. Barbarian mothers do not have ten or twelve

---

* There can no longer be any doubt that the traces which Bachofen thought he had found of unrestricted sexual intercourse, or what he calls 'spontaneous generation in the slime,' [*Sumpfzeugung*], go back to group marriage. 'If Bachofen considers these punaluan marriages "lawless", a man of that period would consider most of the present-day marriages between near and remote cousins on the father's or mother's side to be incestuous, as being marriages between blood brothers and sisters' (Marx).

sons of their own old enough to keep wives in common, but the American system of consanguinity, which corresponds to the punaluan family, provides numerous brothers, because all a man's cousins, near and distant, are his brothers. Caesar's mention of 'parents with children' may be due to misunderstanding on his part; it is not, however, absolutely impossible under this system that father and son or mother and daughter should be included in the same marriage group, though not father and daughter or mother and son. This or a similar form of group marriage also provides the simplest explanation of the accounts in Herodotus and other ancient writers about community of wives among savages and barbarian peoples. The same applies also to the reports of Watson and Kaye in their book, *The People of India*, about the Tikurs in Oudh (north of the Ganges): 'Both sexes have but a nominal tie on each other, and they change connection without compunction; living together, almost indiscriminately, in many large families.'

In the very great majority of cases the institution of the gens seems to have originated directly out of the punaluan family. It is true that the Australian classificatory system also provides an origin for it: the Australians have gentes, but not yet the punaluan family; instead, they have a cruder form of group marriage.

In all forms of group family, it is uncertain who is the father of a child; but it is certain who its mother is. Though she calls *all* the children of the whole family her children and has a mother's duties toward them, she nevertheless knows her own children from the others. It is therefore clear that in so far as group marriage prevails, descent can only be proved on the *mother's* side and that therefore only the *female* line is recognized. And this is in fact the case among all peoples in the period of savagery or in the lower stage of barbarism. It is the second great merit of Bachofen that he was the first to make this discovery. To denote this exclusive recognition of descent through the mother and the relations of inheritance which in time resulted from it, he uses the term 'mother right', which for the sake of brevity I retain. The term is, however, ill-chosen, since at this stage of society there cannot yet be any talk of 'right' in the legal sense.

If we now take one of the two standard groups of the punaluan family, namely a line of natural and collateral sisters (that is, one's own sisters' children in the first, second or more remote degree), together with their children and their own collateral brothers on the mother's side (who, according to our assumption, are *not* their husbands), we have the exact circle of persons whom we later find as members of a gens, in the original form of that institution. They all have a common ancestral mother, by virtue of their descent from whom the female offspring in each generation are sisters. The husbands of these sisters, however, can no longer be their brothers and therefore cannot be descended from the same ancestral mother; consequently, they do not belong to the same consanguine group, the later gens. The children of these sisters, however, do belong to this group, because descent on the mother's side alone counts, since it alone is certain. As soon as the ban had been established on sexual intercourse between all brothers and sisters, including the most remote collateral relatives on the mother's side, this group transformed itself into a gens – that is, it constituted itself as a firm circle of blood relations in the female line between whom marriage was prohibited; and henceforward by other common institutions of a social and religious character, it increasingly consolidated and differentiated itself from the other gentes of the same tribe (more of this later). When we see, then, that the development of the gens follows, not only necessarily, but also perfectly naturally from the punaluan family, we may reasonably infer that at one time this form of family almost certainly existed among all peoples among whom the presence of gentile institutions can be proved – that is, practically all barbarians and civilized peoples.

At the time Morgan wrote his book, our knowledge of group marriage was still very limited. A little information was available about the group marriages of the Australians, who were organized in classes, and Morgan had already in 1871 published the reports he had received concerning the punaluan family in Hawaii. The punaluan family provided, on the one hand, the complete explanation of the system of consanguinity in force among the American Indians, which had been the starting point of all Morgan's researches; on the other hand, the origin of the matriarchal gens could be derived directly from the punaluan family; further the puna- luan family represented a much higher stage of development than the Australian classificatory system. It is therefore comprehensible that Morgan should have regarded it as the necessary stage of development before pairing marriage and should believe it to have been general in earlier times. Since then we have become acquainted with a number of other forms of group marriage, and we now know that Morgan here went too far. However, in his punaluan family he had had the good fortune to strike the highest, the classic form of group marriage, from which the transition to a higher stage can be explained most simply.

For the most important additions to our knowledge of group marriage, we are indebted to the English missionary, Lorimer Fison, who for years studied this form of the family in its classic home, Australia. He found the lowest stage of development among the Australian aborigines of Mount Gambier in South Australia. Here the whole tribe is divided into two great exogamous classes or moieties, Kroki and Kumite. Sexual intercourse within each of these moieties is strictly forbidden; on the other hand, every man in the one moiety is the husband by birth of every woman in the other moiety and she is by birth his wife. Not the individuals, but the entire groups are married, moiety with moiety. And observe that there is no exclusion on the ground of difference in age or particular degrees of affinity, except such as is entailed by the division of the tribe into two exogamous classes. A Kroki has every Kumite woman lawfully to wife; but, as his own daughter according to mother right is also a Kumite, being the daughter of a Kumite woman, she is by birth the wife of every Kroki, including, therefore, her father. At any rate, there is no bar against this in the organization into moieties as we know it. Hence, either this organization arose at a time when, in spite of the obscure impulse toward the restriction of inbreeding, sexual intercourse between parents and children was still not felt to be particularly horrible – in which case the moiety system must have originated directly out of a state of sexual promiscuity – or else intercourse between parents and children was *already* forbidden by custom when the moieties arose – and in that case the present conditions point back to the consanguine family and are the first step beyond it. The latter is more probable. There are not, to my knowledge, any instances from Australia of sexual cohabitation between parents and children, and as a rule the later form of exogamy, the matriarchal gens, also tacitly presupposes the prohibition of this relationship as already in force when the gens came into being.

The system of *two* moieties is found, not only at Mount Gambier in South Australia, but also on the Darling River further to the east and in Queensland in the north-east; it is therefore widely distributed. It excludes marriages only between brothers and sisters, between the children of brothers and between the children of sisters on the mother's side, because these belong to the same moiety; the children of sisters and brothers, however, may marry. A further step toward the prevention of inbreeding was taken by the Kamilaroi on the Darling River in New South Wales; the two original moieties are split up into four, and again each of these four sections is married *en bloc* to another. The first two sections are husbands and wives of one another by birth; according to whether the mother belonged to the first or second section, the children go into the third or fourth; the children of these last two sections, which are also married to one another, come again into the first and second sections. Thus one generation always belongs to the first and second sections, the next to the third and fourth, and the generation after that to the first and second again. Under this system, first cousins (on the mother's side) cannot be man and wife, but second cousins can. This peculiarly complicated arrangement is made still more intricate by having matriarchal gentes grafted onto it (at any rate later), but we cannot go into the details of this now. What is significant is how the urge toward the prevention of inbreeding asserts itself again and again, feeling its way, however, quite instinctively, without clear consciousness of its aim.

Group marriage which in these instances from Australia is still marriage of sections, mass marriage of an entire section of men often scattered over the whole continent with an equally widely distributed section of women – this group marriage, seen close at hand, does not look quite so terrible as the philistines, whose minds cannot get beyond brothels, imagine it to be. On the contrary, for years its existence was not even suspected and has now quite recently been questioned again. All that the superficial observer sees in group marriage is a loose form of monogamous marriage, here and there polygyny, and occasional infidelities. It takes years, as it took Fison and Howitt, to discover beneath these marriage customs, which in their actual practice should seem almost familiar to the average European, their controlling law: the law by which the Australian aborigine, wandering hundreds of miles from his home among people whose language he does not understand, nevertheless often finds in every camp and every tribe women who give themselves to him without resistance and without resentment – the law by which the man with several wives gives one up for the night to his guest. Where the European sees immorality and lawlessness, strict law rules in reality. The women belong to the marriage group of the stranger, and therefore they are his wives by birth; that same law of custom which gives the two to one another forbids under penalty of outlawry all intercourse outside the marriage groups that belong together. Even when wives are captured, as frequently occurs in many places, the law of the exogamous classes is still carefully observed.

Marriage by capture, it may be remarked, already shows signs of the transition to monogamous marriage, at least in the form of pairing marriage. When the young man has captured or abducted a girl with the help of his friends, she is enjoyed by all of them in turn, but afterwards she is regarded as the wife of the young man who instigated her capture. If, on the other hand, the captured woman runs away from her husband and is caught by another man, she becomes his wife and the first husband loses his rights. Thus, while group marriage continues to exist as the general form, side by side with group marriage and within it exclusive relationships begin to form, pairings for a longer or shorter period, also polygyny; thus group marriage is dying out here too, and the only question is which will disappear first under European influence, group marriage or the Australian aborigines who practise it.

Marriage between entire sections, as it prevails in Australia, is in any case a very low and primitive form of group marriage, whereas the punaluan family, so far as we know, represents its highest stage of development. The former appears to be the form corresponding to the social level of vagrant savages, while the latter already presupposes relatively permanent settlements of communistic communities and leads immediately to the successive higher phase of development. But we shall certainly find more than one intermediate stage between these two forms; here lies a newly discovered field of research which is still almost completely unexplored.

3. The Pairing Family

A certain amount of pairing, for a longer or shorter period, already occurred in group marriage or even earlier; the man had a chief wife among his many wives (one can hardly yet speak of a favourite wife), and for her he was the most important among her husbands. This fact has contributed considerably to the confusion of the missionaries, who have regarded group marriage sometimes as promiscuous community of wives, sometimes as unbridled adultery. But these customary pairings were bound to grow more stable as the gens developed and the classes of 'brothers' and 'sisters' between whom marriage was impossible became more numerous. The impulse given by the gens to the prevention of marriage between blood relatives extended still further. Thus among the Iroquois and most of the other Indians at the lower stage of barbarism, we find that marriage is prohibited between *all* relatives enumerated in their system – which includes several hundred degrees of kinship. The increasing complication of these prohibitions made group marriages more and more impossible; they were displaced by the *pairing family*. In this state, one man lives with one woman, but the relationship is such that polygamy and occasional infidelity remain the right of the men, even though for economic reasons polygamy is rare, while from the woman the strictest fidelity is generally demanded throughout the time she lives with the man and adultery on her part is cruelly punished. The marriage tie can, however, be easily dissolved by either partner; after separation, the children still belong as before to the mother alone.

In this ever extending exclusion of blood relatives from the bond of marriage, natural selection continues its work. In Morgan's words:

The influence of the new practice, which brought unrelated persons into the marriage relation, tended to create a more vigorous stock physically and mentally . . . When two advancing tribes, with strong mental and physical characters, are brought together and blended into one people by the accidents of barbarous life, the new skull and brain would widen and lengthen to the sum of the capabilities of both. [p. 468].

Tribes with gentile constitution were thus bound to gain supremacy over more backward tribes, or else to carry them along by their example.

Thus the history of the family in primitive times consists in the progressive narrowing of the circle, originally embracing the whole tribe, within which the two sexes have a common conjugal relation. The continuous exclusion, first of nearer, then of more and more remote relatives, and at last even of relatives by marriage, ends by making any kind of group marriage practically impossible. Finally, there remains only the single, still loosely linked pair, the molecule with whose dissolution marriage itself ceases. This in itself shows what a small part individual sex love, in the modern sense of the word, played in the rise of monogamy. Yet stronger proof is afforded by the practice of all peoples at this stage of development. Whereas in the earlier forms of the family, men never lacked women but, on the contrary, had too many rather than too few, women had now become scarce and highly sought after. Hence it is with the pairing marriage that there begins the capture and purchase of women – widespread *symptoms*, but no more than symptoms, of the much deeper change that had occurred. These symptoms, mere methods of procuring wives, the pedantic Scot McLennan has transmogrified into special classes of families under the names of 'marriage by capture' and 'marriage by purchase'. In general, whether among the American Indians or other peoples (at the same stage), the conclusion of a marriage is the affair not of the two parties concerned, who are often not consulted at all, but of their mothers. Two persons entirely unknown to each other are often thus affianced; they only learn that the bargain has been struck when the time for marrying approaches. Before the wedding the bridegroom gives presents to the bride's gentile relatives (to those on the mother's side, therefore, not to the father and his relations) which are regarded as gift payments in return for the girl. The marriage is still terminable at the desire of either partner, but among many tribes, the Iroquois for example, public opinion has gradually developed against such separations. When differences arise between husband and wife, the gens relatives of both partners act as mediators, and only if these efforts prove fruitless does a separation take place, the wife then keeping the children and each partner being free to marry again.

The pairing family, itself too weak and unstable to make an independent household necessary or even desirable, in no wise destroys the communistic household inherited from earlier times. Communistic housekeeping, however, means the supremacy of women in the house; just as the exclusive recognition of the female parent, owing to the impossibility of recognizing the male parent with certainty, means that the women – the mothers – are held in high respect. One of the most absurd notions taken over from eighteenth-century enlightenment is that in the beginning of society woman was the slave of man. Among all savages and all barbarians of the lower and middle stages, and to a certain extent of the upper stage also, the position of women is not only free, but honourable. As to what it still is in the pairing marriage, let us hear the evidence of Ashur Wright, for many years missionary among the Iroquois Senecas:

As to their family system, when occupying the old long houses [communistic households comprising several families], it is probable that some one clan [gens] predominated, the women taking in husbands, however, from the other clans [gentes] . . . Usually, the female portion ruled the house . . . The stores were in common; but woe to the luckless husband or lover who was too shiftless to do his share of the providing. No matter how many children, or whatever goods he might have in the house, he might at any time be ordered to pick up his blanket and budge; and after such orders it would not be healthful for him to attempt to disobey. The house would be too hot for him; and . . . he must retreat to his own clan [gens]; or, as was often done, go and start a new matrimonial alliance in some other. The women were the great power among the clans [gentes], as everywhere else. They did not hesitate, when occasion required, 'to knock off the horns', as it was technically called, from the head of a chief, and send him back to the ranks of the warriors. [Morgan, p. 464n.].

The communistic household, in which most or all of the women belong to one and the same gens, while the men come from various gentes, is the material foundation of that supremacy of the women which was general in primitive times, and which it is Bachofen's third great merit to have discovered. The reports of travellers and missionaries, I may add, to the effect that women among savages and barbarians are overburdened with work in no way contradict what has been said. The division of labour between the two sexes is determined by quite other causes than by the position of woman in society. Among people where the women have to work far harder than we think suitable, there is often much more real respect for women than among our Europeans. The lady of civilization, surrounded by false homage and estranged from all real work, has an infinitely lower social position than the hard-working woman of barbarism, who was regarded among her people as a real lady (lady, *frowa*, *Frau* – mistress) and who was also a lady in character.

Whether pairing marriage has completely supplanted group marriage in America today is a question to be decided by closer investigation among the peoples still at the upper stage of savagery in the north-west, and particularly in South America. Among the latter, so many instances of sexual licence are related that one can hardly assume the old group marriage to have been completely overcome here. At any rate, all traces of it have not yet disappeared. In at least 40 North American tribes the man who marries an eldest sister has the right to take all her other sisters as his wives as soon as they are old enough – a relic of the time when a whole line of sisters had husbands in common. And Bancroft reports of the Indians of the California peninsula (upper stage of savagery) that they have certain festivals when several 'tribes' come together for the purpose of promiscuous sexual intercourse. These 'tribes' are clearly gentes, who preserve in these feasts a dim memory of the time when the women of one gens had all the men of the other as their common husbands, and conversely. The same custom still prevails in Australia. We find among some peoples that the older men, the chieftains and the magician-priests, exploit the community of wives and monopolize most of the women for themselves; at certain festivals and great assemblies of the people, however, they have to restore the old community of women and allow their wives to enjoy themselves with the young men. Westermarck (*History of Human Marriage*, 1891, pp. 28, 29) quotes a whole series of instances of such periodic Saturnalian feasts when for a short time the old freedom of sexual intercourse is again restored; examples are given among the Hos, the Santals, the Punjas and Kotars in India, among some African peoples, and so forth. Curiously enough, Westermarck draws the conclusion that these are survivals not of the group marriage which he totally rejects, but of the mating season which primitive man had in common with the other animals.

Here we come to Bachofen's fourth great discovery – the widespread transitional form between group marriage and pairing. What Bachofen represents as a penance for the transgression of the old divine laws – the penance by which the woman purchases the right of chastity – is in fact only a mystical expression of the penance by which the woman buys herself out of the old community of husbands and acquires the right to give herself to *one* man only. This penance consists in a limited surrender; the Babylonian women had to give themselves once a year in the temple of Mylitta; other peoples of Asia Minor sent their girls for years to the temple of Anaitis, where they had to practise free love with favourites of their own choosing before they were allowed to marry. Similar customs in religious disguise are common to almost all Asiatic peoples between the Mediterranean and the Ganges. The sacrifice of atonement by which the woman purchases her freedom becomes increasingly lighter in course of time, as Bachofen already noted:

Instead of being repeated annually, the offering is made once only; the hetaerism of the matrons is succeeded by the hetaerism of the maidens; hetaerism during marriage by hetaerism before marriage; surrender to all without choice by surrender to some (*Mutterrecht*, p. xix).

Among other peoples the religious disguise is absent. In some cases – among the Thracians, Celts, and others, in classical times; many of the original inhabitants of India, and to this day among the Malayan peoples, the South Sea Islanders and many American Indians – the girls enjoy the greatest sexual freedom up to the time of their marriage. This is especially the case almost everywhere in South America as everyone who has gone any distance into the interior can testify. Thus Agassiz (*A Journey in Brazil*, Boston and New York, 1868, 266) tells this story of a rich family of Indian extraction. When he was introduced to the daughter, he asked after her father, presuming him to be her mother's husband, who was fighting as an officer in the war against Paraguay; but the mother answered with a smile: *"Naõ tem pai, é filha da fortuna"* (She has no father, she is a child of chance):

It is the way the Indian or half-breed women here always speak of their illegitimate children . . . without an intonation of sadness or of blame . . . So far is this from being an unusual case, that . . . the opposite seems the exception. Children are frequently quite ignorant of their parentage. They know about their mother, for all the care and responsibility falls upon her, but they have no knowledge of their father; nor does it seem to occur to the woman that she or her children have any claim upon him.

What seems strange here to civilized people is simply the rule according to mother right and group marriage.

Among other peoples, again, the friends and relatives of the bridegroom or the wedding guests claim their traditional right to the bride at the wedding itself, and the bridegroom's turn only comes last; this was the custom in the Balearic Islands and among the Augilers of Africa in ancient times; it is still observed among the Bareas of Abyssinia. In other cases, an official personage, the head of the tribe or the gens, *cacique*, shaman, priest, prince or whatever he may be called, represents the community and exercises the right of the first night with the bride. Despite all neo-romantic whitewashing, this *jus primae noctis* (right of first night) still persists today as a relic of group marriage among most of the natives of the Alaska region (Bancroft, *Native Races*, I, p. 81), the Tahus of North Mexico (ibid., p. 584) and other peoples; and at any rate in the countries originally Celtic, where it was handed down directly from group marriage, it existed throughout the whole of the middle ages, for example in Aragon. While in Castile the peasants were never serfs, in Aragon there was serfdom of the most shameful kind right up till the decree of Ferdinand the Catholic in 1486. This document states:

We judge and declare that the aforementioned lords (señors, barons) . . . when the peasant takes himself a wife, shall neither sleep with her on the first night; nor shall they during the wedding night, when the wife has laid herself in her bed, step over it and the aforementioned wife as a sign of lordship; nor shall the aforementioned lords use the daughter or the son of the peasant, with payment or without payment, against their will (quoted in the original Catalan by Sugenheim, *Serfdom*, Petersburg, 1861, p. 35).

Bachofen is also perfectly right when he consistently maintains that the transition from what he calls 'hetaerism' or '*Sumpfzeugung*' to monogamy was brought about primarily through the women. The more the traditional sexual relations lost the naive primitive character of forest life, owing to the development of economic conditions with consequent undermining of the old communism and growing density of population, the more oppressive and humiliating must the women have felt them to be, and the greater their longing for the right of chastity, of temporary or permanent marriage with one man only, as a way of release. This advance could not in any case have originated with the men if only because it has never occurred to them, even to this day, to renounce the pleasures of actual group marriage. Only when the women had brought about the transition to pairing marriage were the men able to introduce strict monogamy – though indeed only for women.

The first beginnings of the pairing family appear on the dividing line between savagery and barbarism; they are generally to be found already at the upper stage of savagery, but occasionally not until the lower stage of barbarism. The pairing family is the form characteristic of barbarism, as group marriage is characteristic of savagery and monogamy of civilization. To develop it further, to strict monogamy, other causes were required than those we have found active hitherto. In the single pair the group was already reduced to its final unit, its two-atom molecule: one man and one woman. Natural selection, with its progressive exclusions from the marriage community, had accomplished its task; there was nothing more for it to do in this direction. Unless new, *social* forces came into play, there was no reason why a new form of family should arise from the single pair. But these new forces did come into play.

We now leave America, the classic soil of the pairing

family. No sign allows us to conclude that a higher form of family developed here or that there was ever permanent monogamy anywhere in America prior to its discovery and conquest. But not so in the Old World.

Here the domestication of animals and the breeding of herds had developed a hitherto unsuspected source of wealth and created entirely new social relations. Up to the lower stage of barbarism, permanent wealth had consisted almost solely of house, clothing, crude ornaments and the tools for obtaining and preparing food – boat, weapons, and domestic utensils of the simplest kind. Food had to be won afresh day by day. Now, with their herds of horses, camels, asses, cattle, sheep, goats, and pigs, the advancing pastoral peoples – the Semites on the Euphrates and the Tigris, and the Aryans in the Indian country of the Five Streams (Punjab), in the Ganges region, and in the steppes then much more abundantly watered by the Oxus and the Jaxartes – had acquired property which only needed supervision and the rudest care to reproduce itself in steadily increasing quantities and to supply the most abundant food in the form of milk and meat. All former means of procuring food now receded into the background; hunting, formerly a necessity, now became a luxury.

But to whom did this new wealth belong? Originally to the gens, without a doubt. Private property in herds must have already started at an early period, however. It is difficult to say whether the author of the so-called first book of Moses regarded the patriarch Abraham as the owner of his herds in his own right as head of a family community or by right of his position as actual hereditary head of a gens. What is certain is that we must not think of him as a property owner in the modern sense of the word. And it is also certain that at the threshold of authentic history we already find the herds everywhere separately owned by heads of families, as are the artistic products of barbarism (metal implements, luxury articles and, finally, the human cattle – the slaves).

For now slavery had also been invented. To the barbarian of the lower stage, a slave was valueless. Hence the treatment of defeated enemies by the American Indians was quite different from that at a higher stage. The men were killed or adopted as brothers into the tribe of the victors; the women were taken as wives or otherwise adopted with their surviving children. At this stage human labour power still does not produce any considerable surplus over and above its maintenance costs. That was no longer the case after the introduction of cattle breeding, metalworking, weaving and, lastly, agriculture. Just as the wives whom it had formerly been so easy to obtain had now acquired an exchange value and were bought, so also with labour power, particularly since the herds had definitely become family possessions. The family did not multiply so rapidly as the cattle. More people were needed to look after them; for this purpose use could be made of the enemies captured in war, who could also be bred just as easily as the cattle themselves.

Once it had passed into the private possession of families and there rapidly begun to augment, this wealth dealt a severe blow to the society founded on pairing marriage and the matriarchal gens. Pairing marriage had brought a new element into the family. By the side of the natural mother of the child it placed its natural and attested father with a better warrant of paternity, probably, than that of many a 'father' today. According to the division of labour within the family at that time, it was the man's part to obtain food and the instruments of labour necessary for the purpose. He therefore also owned the instruments of labour, and in the event of husband and wife separating, he took them with him, just as she retained her household goods. Therefore, according to the social custom of the time, the man was also the owner of the new source of subsistence, the cattle, and later of the new instruments of labour, the slaves. But according to the custom of the same society, his children could not inherit from him. For as regards inheritance, the position was as follows:

At first, according to mother right – so long, therefore, as descent was reckoned only in the female line – and according to the original custom of inheritance within the gens, the gentile relatives inherited from a deceased fellow member of their gens. His property had to remain within the gens. His effects being insignificant, they probably always passed in practice to his nearest gentile relations – that is, to his blood relations on the mother's side. The children of the dead man, however, did not belong to his gens, but to that of their mother; it was from her that they inherited, at first conjointly with her other blood-relations, later perhaps with rights of priority; they could not inherit from their father because they did not belong to his gens within which his property had to remain. When the owner of the herds died, therefore, his herds would go first to his brothers and sisters and to his sister's children, or to the issue of his mother's sisters. But his own children were disinherited.

Thus on the one hand, in proportion as wealth increased it made the man's position in the family more important than the woman's, and on the other hand created an impulse to exploit this strengthened position in order to overthrow, in favour of his children, the traditional order of inheritance. This, however, was impossible so long as descent was reckoned according to mother right. Mother right, therefore, had to be overthrown, and overthrown it was. This was by no means so difficult as it looks to us today. For this revolution – one of the most decisive ever experienced by humanity – could take place without disturbing a single one of the living members of a gens. All could remain as they were. A simple decree sufficed that in the future the offspring of the male members should remain within the gens, but that of the female should be excluded by being transferred to the gens of their father. The reckoning of descent in the female line and the matriarchal law of inheritance were thereby overthrown, and the male line of descent and the paternal law of inheritance were substituted for them. As to how and when this revolution took place among civilized peoples, we have no knowledge. It falls entirely within prehistoric times. But that it *did* take place is more than sufficiently proved by the abundant traces of mother right which have been collected, particularly by Bachofen. How easily it is accomplished can be seen in a whole series of American Indian tribes where it has only recently taken place and is still taking place under the influence, partly of increasing wealth and a changed mode of life (transference from forest to prairie), and partly of the moral pressure of civilization and missionaries. Of eight Missouri tribes, six observe the male line of descent and inheritance; two still observe the female. Among the Shawnees, Miamis and Delawares the custom has grown up of giving the children a gentile name of their father's gens in order to transfer them into it, thus enabling them to inherit from him.

Man's innate casuistry! To change things by changing their names! And to find loopholes for violating tradition while maintaining tradition, when direct interest supplied sufficient impulse (Marx).

The result was hopeless confusion, which could only be remedied and to a certain extent was remedied by the transition to father right. 'In general, this seems to be the most natural transition' (Marx). For the theories proffered by comparative jurisprudence regarding the manner in which this change was effected among the civilized peoples of the Old World – though they are almost pure hypothesis – see M. Kovalevsky (*Tableau des origines et de l'évolution de la famille et de la propriété*, Stockholm, 1890).

The overthrow of mother right was the *world historical defeat of the female sex*. The man took command in the home also; the woman was degraded and reduced to servitude; she became the slave of his lust and a mere instrument for the production of children. This degraded position of the woman, especially conspicuous among the Greeks of the heroic and still more of the classical age, has gradually been palliated and glossed over, and sometimes clothed in a milder form; in no sense has it been abolished.

The establishment of the exclusive supremacy of the man shows its effects first in the patriarchal family, which now emerges as an intermediate form. Its essential characteristic is not polygyny, of which more later, but 'the organization of a number of persons, bond and free, into a family under paternal power for the purpose of holding lands and for the care of flocks and herds ... (In the Semitic form) the chiefs, at least, lived in polygamy ... Those held to servitude and those employed as servants lived in the marriage relation.' [Morgan, p. 474].

Its essential features are the incorporation of unfree persons and paternal power; hence the perfect type of this form of family is the Roman. The original meaning of the word 'family' (*familia*) is not that compound of sentimentality and domestic strife which forms the ideal of the present-day philistine; among the Romans it did not at first even refer to the married pair and their children but only to the slaves. *Famulus* means domestic slave, and *familia* is the total number of slaves belonging to one man. As late as the time of Gaius, the *familia, id est patrimonium* (family, that is, the patrimony, the inheritance) was bequeathed by will. The term was invented by the Romans to denote a new social organism whose head ruled over wife and children and a number of slaves, and was invested under Roman paternal power with rights of life and death over them all.

This term, therefore, is no older than the ironclad family system of the Latin tribes, which came in after field agriculture and after legalized servitude, as well as after the separation of the Greeks and Latins [Morgan, p. 478].

Marx adds:

The modern family contains in germ not only slavery (*servitus*) but also serfdom, since from the beginning it is related to agricultural services. It contains *in miniature* all the contradictions which later extend throughout society and its state.

Such a form of family shows the transition of the pairing family to monogamy. In order to make certain of the wife's fidelity and therefore of the paternity of the children, she is delivered over unconditionally into the power of the husband; if he kills her, he is only exercising his rights.

With the patriarchal family, we enter the field of written history, a field where comparative jurisprudence can give valuable help. And it has in fact brought an important advance in our knowledge. We owe to Maxim Kovalevsky (*Tableau, etc.*, pp. 60–100)[2] the proof that the patriarchal household community, as we still find it today among the Serbs and the Bulgars under the name of *zádruga* (which may be roughly translated 'bond of friendship') or *bratstvo* (brotherhood), and in a modified form among the Oriental peoples, formed the transitional stage between the matriarchal family deriving from group marriage and the single family of the modern world. For the civilized peoples of the Old World, for the Aryans and Semites at any rate, this seems to be established.

The Southern Slav *zádruga* provides the best instance of such a family community still in actual existence. It comprises several generations of the descendants of one father, together with their wives, who all live together in one homestead, cultivate their fields in common, feed and clothe themselves from a common stock, and possess in common the surplus from their labour. The community is under the supreme direction of the head of the house (*domácin*), who acts as its representative outside, has the right to sell minor objects, and controls the funds, for which, as for the regular organization of business, he is responsible. He is elected, and it is not at all necessary that he should be the oldest in the community. The women and their work are under the control of the mistress of the house (*domácica*), who is generally the wife of the *domácin*. She also has an important and often a decisive voice in the choice of husbands for the girls. Supreme power rests, however, with the family council, the assembly of all the adult members of the household, women as well as men. To this assembly the master of the house renders account; it takes all important decisions, exercises jurisdiction over the members, decides on sales and purchases of any importance, especially of land and so on.

It is only within the last ten years or so that such great family communities have been proved to be still in existence

2. M. M. Kovalevsky, *Primitive Law, Book I, Gens*, Moscow, 1886, cites data on the family community in Russia collected by Orshansky in 1875 and Yefimenko in 1878.

in Russia; it is now generally recognized that they are as firmly rooted in the customs of the Russian people as the *obshchina* or village community. They appear in the oldest Russian code of laws, the *Pravda* of Yaroslav, under the same name as in the Dalmatian laws (*vervj*), and references to them can also be traced in Polish and Czech historical sources.

Among the Germans also, according to Heusler (*Institutionen des deutschen Rechts*), the economic unit was originally not the single family in the modern sense but the 'house community', which consisted of several generations or several single families, and often enough included unfree persons as well. The Roman family is now also considered to have originated from this type, and consequently the absolute power of the father of the house and the complete absence of rights among the other members of the family in relation to him have recently been strongly questioned. It is supposed that similar family communities also existed among the Celts in Ireland; in France, under the name of *parçonneries*, they survived in Nivernais until the French Revolution, and in the Franche Comté they have not completely died out even today [1891]. In the district of Louhans (Saône et Loire), large peasant houses can be seen in which live several generations of the same family; the house has a lofty common hall reaching to the roof, and surrounding it the sleeping rooms to which stairs of six or eight steps give access.

In India the household community with common cultivation of the land is already mentioned by Nearchus in the time of Alexander the Great, and it still exists today in the same region, in the Punjab and the whole of north-west India. Kovalevsky was himself able to prove its existence in the Caucasus. In Algeria it survives among the Kabyles. It is supposed to have occurred even in America, and the *calpullis* which Zurita describes in old Mexico have been identified with it; on the other hand, Cunow has proved fairly clearly (in the journal *Ausland*, 1890, nos. 42–4) that in Peru at the time of the conquest there was a form of constitution based on marks (called, curiously enough, *marca*) with periodical allotment of arable land and consequently with individual tillage.

In any case, the patriarchal household community with common ownership and common cultivation of the land now assumes an entirely different significance than hitherto. We can no longer doubt the important part it played as a transitional form between the matriarchal family and the single family among civilized and other peoples of the Old World. Later we will return to the further conclusion drawn by Kovalevsky that it was also the transitional form out of which developed the village or mark community with individual tillage and the allotment, first periodical and then permanent, of arable and pasture land.

With regard to the family life within these communities, it must be observed that at any rate in Russia the master of the house has a reputation for violently abusing his position toward the younger women of the community, especially his daughters-in-law, whom he often converts into his harem; the Russian folk songs have more than a little to say about this.

Before we go on to monogamy, which developed rapidly with the overthrow of mother right, a few words about polygyny and polyandry. Both forms can only be exceptions, historical luxury products as it were, unless they occur side by side in the same country, which is of course not the case. As the men excluded from polygyny cannot console themselves with the women left over from polyandry, and as hitherto, regardless of social institutions, the number of men and women has been fairly equal, it is obviously impossible for either of these forms of marriage to be elevated to the general form. Polygyny on the part of one individual man was, in fact, obviously a product of slavery and confined to a few people in exceptional positions. In the Semitic patriarchal family it was only the patriarch himself, and a few of his sons at most, who lived in polygyny; the rest had to content themselves with one wife. This still holds throughout the whole of the Orient; polygyny is the privilege of the wealthy and of the nobility, the women being recruited chiefly through purchase as slaves; the mass of the people live in monogamy.

A similar exception is the polyandry of India and Tibet, the origin of which in group marriage requires closer examination and would certainly prove interesting. It seems to be much more easy-going in practice than the jealous harems of the Mohammedans. At any rate, among the Nayar in India, where three or four men have a wife in common, each of them can have a second wife in common with another three or more men, and similarly a third and a fourth and so on. It is a wonder that McLennan did not discover in these marriage clubs, to several of which one could belong and which he himself describes, a new class of *club marriage*! This marriage-club system, however, is not real polyandry at all; on the contrary, as Giraud-Teulon has already pointed out, it is a specialized form of group marriage; the men live in polygyny, the women in polyandry.

4. *The Monogamous Family*

It develops out of the pairing family, as previously shown, in the transitional period between the upper and middle stages of barbarism; its decisive victory is one of the signs that civilization is beginning. It is based on the supremacy of the man, the express purpose being to produce children of undisputed paternity; such paternity is demanded because these children are later to come into their father's property as his natural heirs. It is distinguished from pairing marriage by the much greater strength of the marriage tie, which can no longer be dissolved at either partner's wish. As a rule, it is now only the man who can dissolve it and put away his wife. The right of conjugal infidelity also remains secured to him, at any rate by custom (the *Code Napoléon* explicitly accords it to the husband as long as he does not bring his concubine into the house), and as social life develops he exercises his right more and more; should the wife recall the old form of sexual life and attempt to revive it, she is punished more severely than ever.

We meet this new form of the family in all its severity among the Greeks. While the position of the goddesses in their mythology, as Marx points out, refers to an earlier period when the position of women was freer and more respected, in the heroic age we find the woman already being humiliated by the domination of the man and by competition from girl slaves. Note how Telemachus in the *Odyssey* silences his mother. In Homer young women are booty and are handed over to the pleasure of the conquerors, the handsomest being picked by the commanders in order of rank; the entire *Iliad*, it will be remembered, turns on the quarrel of Achilles and Agamemnon over one of these slaves. If a hero is of any importance, Homer also mentions the captive girl with whom he shares his tent and his bed. These girls were also taken back to Greece and brought under the same roof as the wife, as Cassandra was brought by Agamemnon in Aeschylus; the sons begotten of them received a small share of the paternal inheritance and had the full status of freemen. Teucer, for instance, is a natural son of Telamon by one of these slaves and has the right to use his father's name. The legitimate wife was expected to put up with all this, but herself to remain strictly chaste and faithful. In the heroic age a Greek woman is, indeed, more respected than in the period of civilization, but to her husband she is after all nothing but the mother of his legitimate children and heirs, his chief housekeeper and the supervisor of his female slaves, whom he can and does take as concubines if he so fancies. It is the existence of slavery side by side with monogamy, the presence of young, beautiful slaves belonging unreservedly to the *man*, that stamps monogamy from the very beginning with its specific character of monogamy *for the woman only*, but not for the man. And that is the character it still has today.

Coming to the later Greeks, we must distinguish between Dorians and Ionians. Among the former – Sparta is the classic example – marriage relations are in some ways still more archaic than even in Homer. The recognized form of marriage in Sparta was a pairing marriage, modified according to the Spartan conceptions of the state, in which there still survived vestiges of group marriage. Childless marriages were dissolved; King Anaxandridas (about 650 B.C.), whose first wife was childless, took a second and kept two households; about the same time, King Ariston, who had two unfruitful wives, took a third but dismissed one of the other two. On the other hand, several brothers could have a wife in common; a friend who preferred his friend's wife could share her with him; and it was considered quite proper to place one's wife at the disposal of a sturdy 'stallion', as Bismarck would say, even if he was not a citizen. A passage in Plutarch where a Spartan woman refers an importunate wooer to her husband seems to indicate, according to Schömann, even greater freedom. Real adultery, secret infidelity by the woman without the husband's knowledge, was therefore unheard of. On the other hand, domestic slavery was unknown in Sparta, at least during its best period; the unfree helots were segregated on the estates and the Spartans were therefore less tempted to take the helots' wives. Inevitably in these conditions women held a much more honoured position in Sparta than anywhere else in Greece. The Spartan women and the elite of the Athenian *hetaerae* are the only Greek women of whom the ancients speak with respect and whose words they thought it worth while to record.

The position is quite different among the Ionians; here Athens is typical. Girls only learned spinning, weaving, and sewing, and at most a little reading and writing. They lived more or less behind locked doors and had no company except other women. The women's apartments formed a separate part of the house on the upper floor or at the back where men, especially strangers, could not easily enter and to which the women retired when men visited the house. They never went out without being accompanied by a female slave; indoors they were kept under regular guard. Aristophanes speaks of Molossian dogs kept to frighten away adulterers, and, at any rate in the Asiatic towns, eunuchs were employed to keep watch over the women – making and exporting eunuchs was an industry in Chios as early as Herodotus' time, and, according to Wachsmuth, it was not only the barbarians who bought the supply. In Euripides [*Orestes*] a woman is called an *oikurema*, a thing (the word is neuter) for looking after the house, and, apart from her business of bearing children, that was all she was for the Athenian – his chief female domestic servant. The man had his athletics and his public business from which women were barred; in addition, he often had female slaves at his disposal and during the most flourishing days of Athens an extensive system of prostitution which the state at least favoured. It was precisely through this system of prostitution that the only Greek women of personality were able to develop, and to acquire that intellectual and artistic culture by which they stand out as high above the general level of classic womanhood as the Spartan women by their qualities of character. But that a woman had to be a *hetaera* before she could be a woman is the worst condemnation of the Athenian family.

This Athenian family became in time the accepted model for domestic relations not only among the Ionians but to an increasing extent among all the Greeks of the mainland and colonies also. But, in spite of locks and guards, Greek women found plenty of opportunity for deceiving their husbands. The men, who would have been ashamed to show any love for their wives, amused themselves by all sorts of love affairs with *hetaerae*; but this degradation of the women was avenged on the men and degraded them also till they fell into the abominable practice of sodomy and degraded alike their gods and themselves with the myth of Ganymede.

This is the origin of monogamy as far as we can trace it back among the most civilized and highly developed people of antiquity. It was not in any way the fruit of individual sex love, with which it had nothing whatever to do; marriages remained as before marriages of convenience. It was the first form of the family to be based not on natural but on economic conditions – on the victory of private property over primitive, natural communal property. The Greeks themselves put the matter quite frankly: the sole exclusive aims of monogamous marriage were to make the man supreme in the family and to propagate, as the future heirs to his wealth, children indisputably his own. Otherwise, marriage was a burden, a duty which had to be performed whether one liked it or not to gods, state, and one's ancestors. In Athens the law exacted from the man not only marriage but also the performance of a minimum of so-called conjugal duties.

Thus when monogamous marriage first makes its appearance in history, it is not as the reconciliation of man and woman, still less as the highest form of such a reconciliation. Quite the contrary monogamous marriage comes on the scene as the subjugation of the one sex by the other; it announces a struggle between the sexes unknown throughout the whole previous prehistoric period. In an old unpublished manuscript written by Marx and myself in 1846,[3] I find the words: 'The first division of labour is that between man and woman for the propagation of children.' And today I can add: The first class opposition that appears in history coincides with the development of the antagonism between man and woman in monogamous marriage, and the first class oppression coincides with that of the female sex by the male. Monogamous marriage was a great historical step forward; nevertheless, together with slavery and private wealth, it opens the period that has lasted until today in which every step forward is also relatively a step backward, in which prosperity and development for some is won through the misery and frustration of others. It is the cellular form of civilized society in which the nature of the oppositions and contradictions fully active in that society can be already studied.

The old comparative freedom of sexual intercourse by no means disappeared with the victory of pairing marriage or even of monogamous marriage:

The old conjugal system, now reduced to narrower limits by the gradual disappearance of the punaluan groups, still environed the

3. *The German Ideology*, ed. C. J. Arthur (Lawrence & Wishart, London, 1970), p. 51.

advancing family, which it was to follow to the verge of civilization . . . It finally disappeared in the new form of hetaerism, which
still follows mankind in civilization as a dark shadow upon the
family [Morgan, p. 511].

By 'hetaerism' Morgan understands the practice, *coexistent
with monogamous marriage*, of sexual intercourse between men
and unmarried women outside marriage, which, as we know,
flourishes in the most varied forms throughout the whole
period of civilization and develops more and more into open
prostitution. This hetaerism derives quite directly from group
marriage, from the ceremonial surrender by which women
purchased the right of chastity. Surrender for money was at
first a religious act; it took place in the temple of the goddess
of love, and the money originally went into the temple
treasury. The hierodules [temple slaves] of Anaitis in
Armenia and of Aphrodite in Corinth, like the sacred dancing
girls attached to the temples of India, the so-called bayaderes
(the word is a corruption of the Portuguese word *bailadeira*
meaning female dancer), were the first prostitutes. Originally
the duty of every woman, this surrender was later performed
by these priestesses alone as representatives of all other
women. Among other peoples, hetaerism derives from the
sexual freedom allowed girls before marriage – again, therefore, a relic of group marriage, but handed down in a different
way. With the rise of the inequality of property – already at
the upper stage of barbarism, therefore – wage labour appears
sporadically side by side with slave labour, and at the same
time, as its necessary correlate, the professional prostitution
of free women side by side with the forced surrender of the
slave. Thus the heritage which group marriage has
bequeathed to civilization is double-edged, just as everything
civilization brings forth is double-edged, double-tongued,
divided against itself, contradictory: here monogamy, there
hetaerism with its most extreme form, prostitution. For
hetaerism is as much a social institution as any other; it
continues the old sexual freedom – to the advantage of the
men. Actually, not merely tolerated but gaily practised by the

ruling classes particularly, it is condemned in words. But in reality this condemnation never falls on the men concerned, but only on the women; they are despised and outcast in order that the unconditional supremacy of men over the female sex may be once more proclaimed as a fundamental law of society.

But a second contradiction thus develops within monogamous marriage itself. At the side of the husband who embellishes his existence with hetaerism stands the neglected wife. And one cannot have one side of this contradiction without the other, any more than a man has a whole apple in his hand after eating half. But that seems to have been the husbands' notion, until their wives taught them better. With monogamous marriage, two constant social types, unknown hitherto, make their appearance on the scene – the wife's attendant lover and the cuckold husband. The husbands had won the victory over the wives, but the vanquished magnanimously provided the crown. Together with monogamous marriage and hetaerism, adultery became an unavoidable social institution – denounced, severely penalized, but impossible to suppress. At best, the certain paternity of the children rested on moral conviction as before, and to solve the insoluble contradiction the *Code Napoléon*, Article 312, decreed: '*L'enfant conçu pendant le mariage a pour père le mari*' (the father of a child conceived during marriage is – the husband). Such is the final result of three thousand years of monogamous marriage.

Thus wherever the monogamous family remains true to its historical origin and clearly reveals the antagonism between the man and the woman expressed in the man's exclusive supremacy, it exhibits in miniature the same oppositions and contradictions as those in which society has been moving, without power to resolve or overcome them, ever since it split into classes at the beginning of civilization. I am speaking here, of course, only of those cases of monogamous marriage where matrimonial life actually proceeds according to the original character of the whole institution but where the wife rebels against the husband's supremacy. Not all marriages turn out thus, as nobody knows better than the German philistine who can no more assert his rule in the home than he can in the state and whose wife, with every right, wears the trousers he is unworthy of. But, to make up for it, he considers himself far above his French companion in misfortune to whom, oftener than to him, something much worse happens.

However, monogamous marriage did not by any means appear always and everywhere in the classically harsh form it took among the Greeks. Among the Romans, who as future world-conquerors had a larger, if a less fine, vision than the Greeks, women were freer and more respected. A Roman considered that his power of life and death over his wife sufficiently guaranteed her conjugal fidelity. Here, moreover, the wife equally with the husband could dissolve the marriage at will. But the greatest progress in the development of individual marriage certainly came with the entry of the Germans into history, and for the reason that the Germans – on account of their poverty, very probably – were still at a stage where monogamy seems not yet to have become perfectly distinct from pairing marriage. We infer this from three facts mentioned by Tacitus. First, though marriage was held in great reverence – 'they content themselves with one wife, the women live hedged round with chastity' – polygamy was the rule for the distinguished members and the leaders of the tribe, a condition of things similar to that among the Americans, where pairing marriage was the rule. Secondly, the transition from mother right to father right could only have been made a short time previously, for the brother on the mother's side – the nearest gentile male relation according to mother right – was still considered almost closer of kin than the father, corresponding again to the standpoint of the American Indians among whom Marx, as he often said, found the key to the understanding of our own primitive past. And thirdly, women were greatly respected among the Germans and also influential in public affairs, which is in direct contradiction to the supremacy of men in monogamy. In almost all these points the Germans agree with the Spartans, among whom also, as we saw, pairing marriage had not yet been completely overcome. Thus, here again an entirely new influence came to power in the world with the Germans. The new monogamy, which now developed from the mingling of peoples amid the ruins of the Roman world, clothed the supremacy of the men in milder forms and gave women a position which, outwardly at any rate, was much more free and respected than it had ever been in classical antiquity. Only now were the conditions realized in which through monogamy – within it, parallel to it, or in opposition to it, as the case might be – the greatest moral advance we owe to it could be achieved: modern individual sex love, which had hitherto been unknown to the entire world.

This advance, however, undoubtedly sprang from the fact that the Germans still lived in pairing families and grafted the corresponding position of women onto the monogamous system so far as that was possible. It most decidedly did not spring from the legendary virtue and wonderful moral purity of the German character, which was nothing more than the freedom of the pairing family from the crying moral contradictions of monogamy. On the contrary, in the course of their migrations the Germans had morally much deteriorated, particularly during their south-easterly wanderings among the nomads of the Black Sea steppes from whom they acquired not only equestrian skill but also gross, unnatural vices, as Ammianus expressly states of the Taifali and Procopius of the Heruli.

But if monogamy was the only one of all the known forms of the family through which modern sex love could develop, that does not mean that within monogamy modern sexual love developed exclusively or even chiefly as the love of husband and wife for each other. That was precluded by the very nature of strictly monogamous marriage under the rule of the man. Among all historically active classes – that is, among all ruling classes – matrimony remained what it had been since the pairing marriage, a matter of convenience which was arranged by the parents. The first historical form of sexual love as passion, a passion recognized as natural to all human beings (at least if they belonged to the ruling classes), and as the highest form of the sexual impulse – and that is what constitutes its specific character – this first form of individual sexual love, the chivalrous love of the Middle Ages, was by no means conjugal. Quite the contrary, in its classic form among the Provençals, it heads straight for adultery, and the poets of love celebrated adultery. The flower of Provençal love poetry are the Albas [songs of dawn], in German, *Tagelieder*. They describe in glowing colours how the knight lies in bed beside his love – the wife of another – while outside stands the watchman who calls to him as soon as the first grey of dawn (*alba*) appears so that he can get away unobserved; the parting scene then forms the climax of the poem. The northern French and also the worthy Germans adopted this kind of poetry together with the corresponding fashion of chivalrous love; old Wolfram of Eschenbach has left us three wonderfully beautiful songs of dawn on this same improper subject which I like better than his three long heroic poems.

Nowadays there are two ways of concluding a bourgeois marriage. In Catholic countries the parents, as before, procure a suitable wife for their young bourgeois son, and the consequence is, of course, the fullest development of the contradiction inherent in monogamy: the husband abandons himself to hetaerism and the wife to adultery. Probably the only reason why the Catholic Church abolished divorce was because it had convinced itself that there is no more a cure for adultery than there is for death. In Protestant countries, on the other hand, the rule is that the son of a bourgeois family is allowed to choose a wife from his own class with more or less freedom; hence there may be a certain element of love in the marriage as, indeed, in accordance with Protestant hypocrisy is always assumed for decency's sake. Here the husband's hetaerism is a more sleepy kind of business, and adultery by the wife is less the rule. But since in every kind of marriage people remain what they were before and since the bourgeois of Protestant countries are mostly philistines, all that this Protestant monogamy achieves, taking the average of the best cases, is a conjugal partnership of leaden boredom, known as 'domestic bliss'. The best mirror of these two methods of marrying is the novel – the French novel for the Catholic manner, the German for the Protestant. In both, the hero 'gets it': in the German, the young man gets the girl; in the French, the husband gets the horns. Which of them is worse off is sometimes questionable. This is why the French bourgeois is as much horrified by the dullness of the German novel as the German philistine is by the 'immorality' of the French. However, now that 'Berlin is a world capital', the German novel is beginning with a little less timidity to use as part of its regular stock-in-trade the hetaerism and adultery long familiar to that town.

In both cases, however, the marriage is conditioned by the class position of the parties and is to that extent always a marriage of convenience. In both cases this marriage of convenience turns often enough into the crassest prostitution – sometimes of both partners, but far more commonly of the woman, who only differs from the ordinary courtesan in that she does not let out her body on piecework as a wage worker, but sells it once and for all into slavery. And of all marriages of convenience Fourier's words hold true: 'As in grammar two negatives make an affirmative, so in matrimonial morality two prostitutions pass for a virtue.'[4] Sex love in the relationship with a woman becomes and can only become the real rule among the oppressed classes, which means today among the proletariat – whether this relation is officially sanctioned or not. But here all the foundations of typical monogamy are cleared away. Here there is no property, for the preservation and inheritance of which monogamy and male supremacy were established; hence there is no incentive to make this male supremacy effective. What is more, there are no means of making it so. Bourgeois law, which protects this supremacy, exists only for the possessing class and their dealings with the proletarians. The law costs money and, on account of the worker's poverty, it has no validity for his relation to his wife. Here quite other personal and social conditions

4. Charles Fourier, *Théorie de l'Unité Universelle* (Paris, 1841–4), Vol. III, p. 120.

decide. And now that large-scale industry has taken the wife out of the home onto the labour market and into the factory, and made her often the breadwinner of the family, no basis for any kind of male supremacy is left in the proletarian household, except, perhaps, for something of the brutality toward women that has spread since the introduction of monogamy. The proletarian family is therefore no longer monogamous in the strict sense, even where there is passionate love and firmest loyalty on both sides and maybe all the blessings of religious and civil authority. Here, therefore, the eternal attendants of monogamy, hetaerism and adultery, play only an almost vanishing part. The wife has in fact regained the right to dissolve the marriage, and if two people cannot get on with one another, they prefer to separate. In short, proletarian marriage is monogamous in the etymological sense of the word, but not at all in its historical sense.

Our jurists, of course, find that progress in legislation is leaving women with no further ground of complaint. Modern civilized systems of law increasingly acknowledge first, that for a marriage to be legal it must be a contract freely entered into by both partners and secondly, that also in the married state both partners must stand on a common footing of equal rights and duties. If both these demands are consistently carried out, say the jurists, women have all they can ask.

This typically legalist method of argument is exactly the same as that which the radical republican bourgeois uses to put the proletarian in his place. The labour contract is to be freely entered into by both partners. But it is considered to have been freely entered into as soon as the law makes both parties equal on *paper*. The power conferred on the one party by the difference of class position, the pressure thereby brought to bear on the other party – the real economic position of both – that is not the law's business. Again, for the duration of the labour contract, both parties are to have equal rights in so far as one or the other does not expressly surrender them. That economic relations compel the worker to surrender even the last semblance of equal rights – here again, that is no concern of the law.

In regard to marriage, the law, even the most advanced, is fully satisfied as soon as the partners have formally recorded that they are entering into the marriage of their own free consent. What goes on in real life behind the juridical scenes, how this free consent comes about – that is not the business of the law and the jurist. And yet the most elementary comparative jurisprudence should show the jurist what this free consent really amounts to. In the countries where an obligatory share of the paternal inheritance is secured to the children by law and they cannot therefore be disinherited – in Germany, in the countries with French law and elsewhere – the children are obliged to obtain their parents' consent to their marriage. In the countries with English law, where parental consent to a marriage is not legally required, the parents on their side have full freedom in the testamentary disposal of their property and can disinherit their children at their pleasure. It is obvious that in spite and precisely because of this fact freedom of marriage among the classes with something to inherit is in reality not a whit greater in England and America than it is in France and Germany.

As regards the legal equality of husband and wife in marriage, the position is no better. The legal inequality of the two partners bequeathed to us from earlier social conditions is not the cause but the effect of the economic oppression of the woman. In the old communistic household, which comprised many couples and their children, the task entrusted to the women of managing the household was as much a public, a socially necessary industry as the procuring of food by the men. With the patriarchal family and still more with the single monogamous family, a change came. Household management lost its public character. It no longer concerned society. It became a *private service*; the wife became the head servant, excluded from all participation in social production. Not until the coming of modern large-scale industry was the road to social production opened to her again – and then only to the proletarian wife. But it was opened in such a manner that, if she carries out her duties in the private service of her family, she remains excluded from public production and unable to earn; and if she wants to take part in public production and earn independently, she cannot carry out family duties. And the wife's position in the factory is the position of women in all branches of business, right up to medicine and the law. The modern individual family is founded on the open or concealed domestic slavery of the wife, and modern society is a mass composed of these individual families as its molecules.

In the great majority of cases today, at least in the possessing classes, the husband is obliged to earn a living and support his family, and that in itself gives him a position of supremacy without any need for special legal titles and privileges. Within the family he is the bourgeois, and the wife represents the proletariat. In the industrial world, the specific character of the economic oppression burdening the proletariat is visible in all its sharpness only when all special legal privileges of the capitalist class have been abolished and complete legal equality of both classes established. The democratic republic does not do away with the opposition of the two classes; on the contrary, it provides the clear field on which the fight can be fought out. And in the same way, the peculiar character of the supremacy of the husband over the wife in the modern family, the necessity of creating real social equality between them and the way to do it, will only be seen in the clear light of day when both possess legally complete equality of rights. Then it will be plain that the first condition for the liberation of the wife is to bring the whole female sex back into public industry, and that this in turn demands that the characteristic of the monogamous family as the economic unit of society be abolished.

We thus have three principal forms of marriage which correspond broadly to the three principal stages of human development: for the period of savagery, group marriage; for barbarism, pairing marriage; for civilization, monogamy supplemented by adultery and prostitution. Between pairing marriage and monogamy intervenes a period in the upper stage of barbarism when men have female slaves at their command and polygamy is practised.

As our whole presentation has shown, the progress which manifests itself in these successive forms is connected with the peculiarity that women, but not men, are increasingly deprived of the sexual freedom of group marriage. In fact, for men group marriage actually still exists even to this day. What for the woman is a crime entailing grave legal and social consequences is considered honourable in a man or, at the worst, a slight moral blemish which he cheerfully bears. But the more the hetaerism of the past is changed in our time by capitalist commodity production and brought into conformity with it, the more, that is to say, it is transformed into undisguised prostitution, the more demoralizing are its effects. And it demoralizes men far more than women. Among women, prostitution degrades only the unfortunate ones who become its victims, and even these by no means to the extent commonly believed. But it degrades the character of the whole male world. A long engagement particularly is in nine cases out of ten a regular preparatory school for conjugal infidelity.

We are now approaching a social revolution in which the economic foundations of monogamy as they have existed hitherto will disappear just as surely as those of its complement – prostitution. Monogamy arose from the concentration of considerable wealth in the hands of a single individual – a man – and from the need to bequeath this wealth to the children of that man and of no other. For this purpose, the monogamy of the woman was required, not that of the man, so this monogamy of the woman did not in any way interfere with open or concealed polygamy on the part of the man. But by transforming by far the greater portion, at any rate, of permanent, heritable wealth – the means of production – into social property, the coming social revolution will reduce to a minimum all this anxiety about bequeathing and inheriting. Having arisen from economic causes, will monogamy then disappear when these causes disappear?

One might answer, not without reason: far from disappearing, it will on the contrary begin to be realized completely. For with the transformation of the means of production into social property there will disappear also wage labour, the proletariat, and therefore the necessity for a certain – statistically calculable – number of women to surrender themselves for money. Prostitution disappears; monogamy, instead of collapsing, at last becomes a reality – also for men.

In any case, therefore, the position of men will be very much altered. But the position of women, of *all* women, also undergoes significant change. With the transfer of the means of production into common ownership, the single family ceases to be the economic unit of society. Private housekeeping is transformed into a social industry. The care and education of the children becomes a public affair; society looks after all children alike, whether they are legitimate or not. This removes all the anxiety about the 'consequences', which today is the most essential social – moral as well as economic – factor that prevents a girl from giving herself completely to the man she loves. Will not that suffice to bring about the gradual growth of unconstrained sexual intercourse and with it a more tolerant public opinion in regard to a maiden's honour and a woman's shame? And finally, have we not seen that in the modern world monogamy and prostitution are indeed contradictions, but inseparable contradictions, poles of the same state of society? Can prostitution disappear without dragging monogamy with it into the abyss?

Here a new element comes into play, an element which at the time when monogamy was developing existed at most in embryo – individual sex love.

Before the Middle Ages we cannot speak of individual sex love. That personal beauty, close intimacy, similarity of tastes and so forth awakened in people of opposite sex the desire for sexual intercourse, that men and women were not totally indifferent regarding the partner with whom they entered into this most intimate relationship – that goes without saying. But it is still a very long way to our sexual love. Throughout the whole of antiquity, marriages were arranged by the parents, and the partners calmly accepted their choice. What little love there was between husband and wife in antiquity is not so much subjective inclination as objective duty, not the cause of the marriage but its corollary. Love relationships in the modern sense only occur in antiquity outside official society. The shepherds of whose joy and sorrows in love Theocritus and Moschus sing, the Daphnis and Chloe of Longus, are all slaves who have no part in the state, the free citizen's sphere of life. Except among slaves, we find love affairs only as products of the disintegration of the old world and carried on with women who also stand outside official society, with *hetaerae* – that is, with foreigners or freed slaves: in Athens from the eve of its decline, in Rome under the Caesars. If there were any real love affairs between free men and free women, these occurred only in the course of adultery. And to the classical love poet of antiquity, old Anacreon, sexual love in our sense mattered so little that it did not even matter to him which sex his beloved was.

Our sex love differs essentially from the simple sexual desire, the Eros, of the ancients. In the first place, it assumes that the person loved returns the love; to this extent the woman is on an equal footing with the man, whereas in the Eros of antiquity she was often not even asked. Secondly, our sex love has a degree of intensity and duration which makes both lovers feel that non-possession and separation are a great, if not the greatest, calamity; to possess one another, they risk high stakes, even life itself. In the ancient world this happened only, if at all, in adultery. And finally, there arises a new moral standard in the judgement of a sexual relationship. We do not only ask, was it within or outside marriage, but also, did it spring from love and reciprocated love or not? Of course, this new standard has fared no better in feudal or bourgeois practice than all the other standards of morality – it is ignored. But neither does it fare any worse. It is recognized, like all the rest, in theory, on paper. And for the present more than this cannot be expected.

At the point where antiquity broke off its advance to sexual love, the Middle Ages took it up again – in adultery. We have already described the knightly love which gave rise to the songs of dawn. From the love which strives to break up marriage to the love which is to be its foundation there is still a long road, which chivalry never fully traversed. Even when we pass from the frivolous Latins to the virtuous Germans we find in the *Nibelungenlied* that although in her heart Kriemhild is as much in love with Siegfried as he is with her, yet when Gunther announces that he has promised her to a knight he does not name, she simply replies: 'You have no need to ask me; as you bid me, so will I ever be; whom you, lord, give me as husband, him will I gladly take in troth.' It never enters her head that her love can be even considered. Gunther asks for Brünhild in marriage and Etzel for Kriemhild, though they have never seen them. Similarly, in *Gutrun*, Sigebant of Ireland asks for the Norwegian Ute, whom he has never seen, Hetel of Hegelingen for Hilde of Ireland, and finally Siegfried of Morland, Hartmut of Ormany and Herwig of Seeland for Gutrun – and here Gutrun's acceptance of Herwig is for the first time voluntary. As a rule, the young prince's bride is selected by his parents if they are still living or, if not, by the prince himself with the advice of the great feudal lords, who have a weighty word to say in all these cases. Nor can it be otherwise. For the knight or baron, as for the prince of the land himself, marriage is a political act, an opportunity to increase power by new alliances; the interest of the *house* must be decisive, not the wishes of an individual. What chance then is there for love to have the final word in the making of a marriage?

The same thing holds for the guild member in the medieval towns. The very privileges protecting him, the guild charters with all their clauses and rubrics, the intricate distinctions legally separating him from other guilds, from the members of his own guild or from his journeymen and apprentices, already made the circle narrow enough within which he could look for a suitable wife. And who in the circle was the most suitable was decided under this complicated system most certainly not by his individual preference but by the family interests.

In the vast majority of cases, therefore, marriage remained up to the close of the Middle Ages what it had been from the start – a matter which was not decided by the partners. In the beginning, people were already born married – married to an entire group of the opposite sex. In the later forms of group marriage similar relations probably existed, but with the group continually contracting. In the pairing marriage it was customary for the mothers to settle the marriages of their children; here, too, the decisive considerations are the new ties of kinship which are to give the young pair a stronger position in the gens and tribe. And when, with the preponderance of private over communal property and the interest in its bequeathal father right and monogamy gained supremacy, the dependence of marriages on economic considerations became complete. The *form* of marriage by purchase disappears; the actual practice is steadily extended until not only the woman but also the man acquires a price – not according to his personal qualities but according to his property. That the mutual affection of the people concerned should be the one paramount reason for marriage, outweighing everything else, was and always had been absolutely unheard of in the practice of the ruling classes; that sort of thing only happened in romance – or among the oppressed classes, who did not count.

Such was the state of things encountered by capitalist production when it began to prepare itself, after the epoch of geographical discoveries, to win world power by world trade and manufacture. One would suppose that this manner of marriage exactly suited it, and so it did. And yet – there are no limits to the irony of history – capitalist production itself was to make the decisive breach in it. By changing all things into commodities, it dissolved all inherited and traditional relationships, and in place of time-honoured custom and historic right, it set up purchase and sale, 'free' contract. And the English jurist H. S. Maine thought he had made a tremendous discovery when he said that our whole progress in comparison with former epochs consisted in the fact that we had passed 'from status to contract', from inherited to freely contracted conditions – which, in so far as it is correct was already in *The Communist Manifesto* [Chapter II].

But a contract requires people who can dispose freely of their persons, actions, and possessions and meet each other on the footing of equal rights. To create these 'free' and 'equal' people was one of the main tasks of capitalist production. Even though at the start it was carried out only half-consciously, and under a religious disguise at that, from the time of the Lutheran and Calvinist Reformation the principle was established that man is only fully responsible for his actions when he acts with complete freedom of will, and that it is a moral duty to resist all coercion to an immoral act. But how did this fit in with the hitherto existing practice in the arrangement of marriages? Marriage according to the bourgeois conception was a contract, a legal transaction, and the most important one of all because it disposed of two human beings, body and mind, for life. Formally, it is true, the contract at that time was entered into voluntarily; without the assent of the persons concerned, nothing could be done. But everyone knew only too well how this assent was obtained and who were the real contracting parties in the marriage. But if real freedom of decision was required for all other contracts, then why not for this? Had not the two young people to be coupled also the right to dispose freely of themselves, of their bodies and organs? Had not chivalry brought sex love into fashion, and was not its proper bourgeois form, in contrast to chivalry's adulterous love, the love of husband and wife? And if it was the duty of married people to love each other, was it not equally the duty of lovers to marry each other and nobody else? Did not this right of the lovers stand higher than the right of parents, relations, and other traditional marriage brokers and matchmakers? If the right of free, personal discrimination broke boldly into the Church and religion, how should it halt before the intolerable claim of the older generation to dispose of the body, soul, property, happiness, and unhappiness of the younger generation?

These questions inevitably arose at a time which was

loosening all the old ties of society and undermining all traditional conceptions. The world had suddenly grown almost ten times bigger; instead of one quadrant of a hemisphere, the whole globe lay before the gaze of the West Europeans who hastened to take the other seven quadrants into their possession. And with the old narrow barriers of their homeland fell also the thousand-year-old barriers of the prescribed medieval way of thought. To the outward and the inward eye of man opened an infinitely wider horizon. What did a young man care about the approval of respectability or honourable guild privileges handed down for generations when the wealth of India beckoned to him, the gold and the silver mines of Mexico and Potosi? For the bourgeoisie it was the time of knight-errantry; they, too, had their romance and their raptures of love, but on a bourgeois footing and, in the last analysis, with bourgeois aims.

So it came about that the rising bourgeoisie, especially in Protestant countries where existing conditions had been most severely shaken, increasingly recognized freedom of contract also in marriage, and carried it into effect in the manner described. Marriage remained class marriage, but within the class the partners were conceded a certain degree of freedom of choice. And on paper, in ethical theory and in poetic description, nothing was more immutably established than that every marriage is immoral which does not rest on mutual sexual love and really free agreement of husband and wife. In short, the love marriage was proclaimed as a human right, and indeed not only as a *droit de l'homme*, one of the rights of man, but also, for once in a way, as *droit de la femme*, one of the rights of woman.

This human right, however, differed in one respect from all other so-called human rights. While the latter in practice remain restricted to the ruling class (the bourgeoisie) and are directly or indirectly curtailed for the oppressed class (the proletariat), in the case of the former the irony of history plays another of its tricks. The ruling class remains dominated by the familiar economic influences and therefore only in exceptional cases does it provide instances of really freely contracted marriages, while among the oppressed class, as we have seen, these marriages are the rule.

Full freedom of marriage can therefore only be generally established when the abolition of capitalist production and of the property relations created by it has removed all the accompanying economic considerations which still exert such a powerful influence on the choice of a marriage partner. For then there is no other motive left except mutual inclination.

And as sexual love is by its nature exclusive – although at present this exclusiveness is fully realized only in the woman – the marriage based on sexual love is by its nature individual marriage. We have seen how right Bachofen was in regarding the advance from group marriage to individual marriage as primarily due to the women. Only the step from pairing marriage to monogamy can be put down to the credit of the men, and historically the essence of this was to make the position of the women worse and the infidelities of the men easier. If now the economic considerations also disappear which made women put up with the habitual infidelity of their husbands – concern for their own means of existence and still more for their children's future – then, according to all previous experience, the equality of women thereby achieved will tend infinitely more to make men really monogamous than to make women polyandrous.

But what will quite certainly disappear from monogamy are all the features stamped upon it through its origin in property relations; these are, in the first place, supremacy of the man and secondly, the indissolubility of marriage. The supremacy of the man in marriage is the simple consequence of his economic supremacy, and with the abolition of the latter will disappear of itself. The indissolubility of marriage is partly a consequence of the economic situation in which monogamy arose, partly tradition from the period when the connection between this economic situation and monogamy was not yet fully understood and was carried to extremes under a religious form. Today it is already broken through at a thousand points. If only the marriage based on love is moral, then also only the marriage is moral in which love continues. But the intense emotion of individual sex love varies very much in duration from one individual to another, especially among men, and if affection definitely comes to an end or is supplanted by a new passionate love, separation is a benefit for both partners as well as for society – only people will then be spared having to wade through the useless mire of a divorce case.

What we can now conjecture about the way in which sexual relations will be ordered after the impending overthrow of capitalist production is mainly of a negative character, limited for the most part to what will disappear. But what will there be new? That will be answered when a new generation has grown up: a generation of men who never in their lives have known what it is to buy a woman's surrender with money or any other social instrument of power; a generation of women who have never known what it is to give themselves to a man from any other considerations than real love or to refuse to give themselves to their lover from fear of the economic consequences. When these people are in the world, they will care precious little what anybody today thinks they ought to do; they will make their own practice and their corresponding public opinion about the practice of each individual – and that will be the end of it.

Let us, however, return to Morgan, from whom we have moved a considerable distance. The historical investigation of the social institutions developed during the period of civilization goes beyond the limits of his book. How monogamy fares during this epoch, therefore, only occupies him very briefly. He, too, sees in the further development of the monogamous family a step forward, an approach to complete equality of the sexes, though he does not regard this goal as attained. But, he says:

When the fact is accepted that the family has passed through four successive forms and is now in a fifth, the question at once arises whether this form can be permanent in the future. The only answer that can be given is that it must advance as society advances, and change as society changes, even as it has done in the past. It is the creature of the social system, and will reflect its culture. As the monogamian family has improved greatly since the commencement of civilization, and very sensibly in modern times, it is at least supposable that it is capable of still further improvement until the equality of the sexes is attained. Should the monogamian family in the distant future fail to answer the requirements of society . . . it is impossible to predict the nature of its successor [p. 499].

CHAPTER III

The Iroquois Gens

We now come to another discovery made by Morgan, which is at least as important as the reconstruction of the family in its primitive form from the systems of consanguinity. The proof that the kinship organizations designated by animal names in a tribe of American Indians are essentially identical with the *genea* of the Greeks and the *gentes* of the Romans; that the American is the original form and the Greek and Roman forms are later and derivative; that the whole social organization of the primitive Greeks and Romans into gens, phratry, and tribe finds its faithful parallel in that of the American Indians; that the gens is an institution common to all barbarians until their entry into civilization and even afterward (so far as our sources go up to the present) – this proof has cleared up at one stroke the most difficult questions in the most ancient periods of Greek and Roman history, providing us at the same time with an unsuspected wealth of information about the fundamental features of social constitution in primitive times, before the introduction of the *state*. Simple as the matter seems once it is understood, Morgan only made his discovery quite recently. In his previous work, published in 1871,[5] he had not yet penetrated this secret, at whose subsequent revelation the English anthropologists, usually so self-confident, became for a time as quiet as mice.

The Latin word *gens*, which Morgan uses as a general term for such kinship organizations, comes, like its Greek equivalent, *genos*, from the common Aryan root *gan* (in German,

5. *Systems of Consanguinity and Affinity of the Human Family* (Smithsonian Publications, 1871).

116

where following the law Aryan *g* is regularly replaced by *k*, *kan*), which means to beget. *Gens, genos*, Sanscrit *jánas*, Gothic *kuni* (following the same law as above), Old Norse and Anglo-Saxon *kyn*, English *kin*, Middle High German *künne*, all signify lineage, descent. *Gens* in Latin and *genos* in Greek are, however, used specifically to denote the form of kinship organization which prides itself on its common descent (in this case from a common ancestral father) and is bound together by social and religious institutions into a distinct community, though to all our historians its origin and character have hitherto remained obscure.

We have already seen in connection with the punaluan family what is the composition of a gens in its original form. It consists of all the persons who in punaluan marriage, according to the conceptions necessarily prevailing under it, form the recognized descendants of one particular ancestral mother, the founder of the gens. In this form of family, as paternity is uncertain, only the female line counts. Since brothers may not marry their sisters but women of different descent, the children begotten by them with these alien women cannot according to mother right belong to the father's gens. Therefore only the offspring of the *daughters* in each generation remain within the kinship organization; the offspring of the sons go into the gentes of their mothers. What becomes of this consanguine group when it has constituted itself a separate group distinct from similar groups within the tribe?

As the classic form of this original gens, Morgan takes the gens among the Iroquois and especially in the Seneca tribe. In this tribe there are eight gentes, named after animals: (1) Wolf, (2) Bear, (3) Turtle, (4) Beaver, (5) Deer, (6) Snipe, (7) Heron, (8) Hawk. In every gens the following customs are observed:

1. The gens elects its sachem (head of the gens in peace) and its chief (leader in war). The sachem had to be chosen from among the members of the gens, and his office was hereditary within the gens in the sense that it had to be filled immediately as often as a vacancy occurred. The military

leader could be chosen from outside the gens, and for a time the office might even be vacant. A son was never chosen to succeed his father as sachem since mother right prevailed among the Iroquois, and the son consequently belonged to a different gens; but the office might and often did pass to a brother of the previous sachem or to his sister's son. All voted in the elections, both men and women. The election, however, still required the confirmation of the seven remaining gentes, and only then was the new sachem ceremonially invested with his office by the common council of the whole Iroquois confederacy. The significance of this will appear later. The authority of the sachem within the gens was paternal and purely moral in character; he had no means of coercion. By virtue of his office he was also a member of the tribal council of the Senecas and also of the federal council of all the Iroquois. The war chief could only give orders on military expeditions.

2. The gens deposes the sachem and war chief at will. This also is done by men and women jointly. After a sachem or chief had been deposed, they became simple braves, private persons, like the other members. The tribal council also had the power to depose sachems, even against the will of the gens.

3. No member is permitted to marry within the gens. This is the fundamental law of the gens, the bond which holds it together. It is the negative expression of the very positive blood relationship by virtue of which the individuals it comprises become a gens. By his discovery of this simple fact Morgan has revealed for the first time the nature of the gens. How little the gens was understood before is obvious from the earlier reports about savages and barbarians in which the various bodies out of which the gentile organization is composed are ignorantly and indiscriminately referred to as tribe, clan, *thum*, and so forth, and then sometimes designated as bodies within which marriage is prohibited. Thus was created the hopeless confusion which gave Mr McLennan his chance to appear as Napoleon, establishing order by his decree: All tribes are divided into those within which

marriage is prohibited (exogamous) and those within which it is permitted (endogamous). Having now made the muddle complete, he could give himself up to the profoundest inquiries as to which of his two absurd classes was the older – exogamy or endogamy. All this nonsense promptly stopped of itself with the discovery of the gens and of its basis in consanguinity, involving the exclusion of its members from intermarriage with one another. Obviously, at the stage at which we find the Iroquois the prohibition of marriage within the gens was stringently observed.

4. The property of deceased persons passed to the other members of the gens; it had to remain in the gens. As an Iroquois had only things of little value to leave, the inheritance was shared by his nearest gentile relations; in the case of a man, by his own brothers and sisters and maternal uncle; in the case of a woman, by her children and own sisters, but not by her brothers. For this reason man and wife could not inherit from one another, nor children from their father.

5. The members of the gens owed each other help, protection, and especially assistance in avenging injury by strangers. The individual looked for his security to the protection of the gens and could rely upon receiving it; to wrong him was to wrong his whole gens. From the bonds of blood uniting the gens sprang the obligation of blood revenge, which the Iroquois unconditionally recognized. If any person from outside the gens killed a gentile member, the obligation of blood revenge rested on the entire gens of the slain man. First, mediation was tried; the gens of the slayer sat in council and made proposals of settlement to the council of the gens of the slain, usually offering expressions of regret and presents of considerable value. If these were accepted, the matter was disposed of. In the contrary case, the wronged gens appointed one or more avengers whose duty it was to pursue and kill the slayer. If this was accomplished, the gens of the slayer had no ground of complaint; accounts were even and closed.

6. The gens has special names or classes of names which may not be used by any other gens in the whole tribe, so that

the name of the individual indicates the gens to which he belongs. A gentile name confers of itself gentile rights.

7. The gens can adopt strangers and thereby admit them into the whole tribe. Thus among the Senecas the prisoners of war who were not killed became through adoption into a gens members of the tribe, receiving full gentile and tribal rights. The adoption took place on the proposal of individual members of the gens; if a man adopted, he accepted the stranger as brother or sister; if a woman, as son or daughter. The adoption had to be confirmed by ceremonial acceptance into the tribe. Frequently, a gens which was exceptionally reduced in numbers was replenished by mass adoption from another gens, with its consent. Among the Iroquois the ceremony of adoption into the gens was performed at a public council of the tribe and therefore was actually a religious rite.

8. Special religious ceremonies can hardly be found among the Indian gentes; the religious rites of the Indians are, however, more or less connected with the gens. At the six yearly religious festivals of the Iroquois, the sachems and war chiefs of the different gentes were included *ex officio* among the 'Keepers of the Faith' and had priestly functions.

9. The gens has a common burial place. Among the Iroquois of New York State, who are hedged in on all sides by white people, this has disappeared, but it existed formerly. It exists still among other Indians – for example, among the Tuscaroras, who are closely related to the Iroquois; although they are Christians, each gens has a separate row in the cemetery; the mother is therefore buried in the same row as her children, but not the father. And among the Iroquois also the whole gens of the deceased attends the burial, prepares the grave, delivers funeral addresses, and so forth.

10. The gens has a council, the democratic assembly of all male and female adult gentiles, all with equal votes. This council elected sachems, war chiefs and also the other 'Keepers of the Faith' and deposed them. It took decisions regarding blood revenge or payment of atonement for murdered gentiles; it adopted strangers into the gens. In short, it was the sovereign power in the gens.

Such were the rights and privileges of a typical Indian gens.

All the members of an Iroquois gens were personally free, and they were bound to defend each other's freedom; they were equal in privileges and in personal rights, the sachem and chiefs claiming no superiority; and they were a brotherhood bound together by the ties of kin. Liberty, equality, and fraternity, though never formulated, were cardinal principles of the gens. These facts are material, because the gens was the unit of a social and governmental system, the foundation upon which Indian society was organized . . . It serves to explain that sense of independence and personal dignity universally an attribute of Indian character [pp. 85–6].

The Indians of the whole of North America at the time of its discovery were organized in gentes under mother right. The gentes had disappeared only in some tribes, as among the Dakotas; in others, as among the Ojibwas and the Omahas, they were organized according to father right.

Among very many Indian tribes with more than five or six gentes, we find every three, four, or more gentes united in a special group which Morgan, rendering the Indian name faithfully by its Greek equivalent, calls a 'phratry' (brotherhood). Thus the Senecas have two phratries: the first comprises gentes (1) to (4), the second gentes (5) to (8). Closer investigation shows that these phratries generally represent the original gentes into which the tribe first split up; for since marriage was prohibited within the gens, there had to be at least two gentes in any tribe to enable it to exist independently. In the measure in which the tribe increased, each gens divided again into two or more gentes, each of which now appears as a separate gens, while the original gens, which includes all the daughter gentes, continues as the phratry.

Among the Senecas and most other Indians, the gentes within one phratry are brother gentes to one another while those in the other phratry are their cousin gentes – terms which in the American system of consanguinity have, as we have seen, a very real and expressive meaning. Originally no Seneca was allowed to marry within his phratry, but this restriction has long since become obsolete and is now confined to the gens. According to Senecan tradition, the Bear and the Deer were the two original gentes from which the others branched off. After this new institution had once taken firm root, it was modified as required; if the gentes in one phratry died out, entire gentes were sometimes transferred into it from other phratries to make the numbers even. Hence we find gentes of the same name grouped in different phratries in different tribes.

Among the Iroquois the functions of the phratry are partly social, partly religious. (1) In the ball game one phratry plays against another. Each phratry puts forward its best players, while the other members, grouped according to phratries, look on and bet against one another on the victory of their players. (2) In the tribal council the sachems and the war chiefs of each phratry sit together, the two groups facing one another; each speaker addresses the representatives of each phratry as a separate body. (3) If a murder had been committed in the tribe and the slayer and the slain belonged to different phratries, the injured gens often appealed to its brother gentes; these held a council of the phratry and appealed in a body to the other phratry that it also should assemble its council to effect a settlement. Here the phratry reappears as the original gens and with greater prospect of success than the weaker single gens, its offspring. (4) At the death of prominent persons the opposite phratry saw to the interment and the burial ceremonies, while the phratry of the dead person attended as mourners. If a sachem died, the opposite phratry reported to the federal council of the Iroquois that the office was vacant. (5) The council of the phratry also played a part in the election of a sachem. That the election would be confirmed by the brother gentes was more or less taken for granted, but the gentes of the opposite phratry might raise an objection. In this case the council of the opposite phratry was assembled; if it maintained the objection, the election was void. (6) The Iroquois formerly had special religious mysteries, called medicine lodges by the white men. Among the Senecas, these mysteries were celebrated by two religious brotherhoods into which new members were admitted by formal initiation; there was one such brotherhood in each of the two phratries. (7) If, as is almost certain, the four lineages occupying the four quarters of Tlascalá at the time of the Conquest [of Mexico] were four phratries, we here have proof that the phratries were also military units, like the phratries among the Greeks and similar kinship organizations among the Germans; these four lineages went into battle as separate groups each with its own uniform and flag and under its own leader.

As several gentes make up a phratry, so in the classic form several phratries make up a tribe; in some cases, when tribes have been much weakened, the intermediate form, the phratry, is absent. What distinguishes an Indian tribe in America?

1. *Its own territory and name.* In addition to its actual place of settlement, every tribe further possessed considerable territory for hunting and fishing. Beyond that lay a broad strip of neutral land reaching to the territory of the neighbouring tribe; it was smaller between tribes related in language, larger between tribes not so related. It is the same as the boundary forest of the Germans, the waste made by Caesar's Suevi around their territory, the *isarnholt* (in Danish, *jarnved, limes Danicus*) between Danes and Germans, the Saxon forest, and the *branibor* (Slav, 'protecting wood') between Germans and Slavs, from which Brandenburg takes its name. The territory delimited by these uncertain boundaries was the common land of the tribe, recognized as such by neighbouring tribes and defended by the tribe itself against attacks. In most cases the uncertainty of the boundaries only became a practical disadvantage when there had been a great increase in population. The names of the tribes seem generally to have arisen by chance rather than to have been deliberately chosen; in the course of time it often happened that a tribe was called by another name among the neighbouring tribes than that which it used itself, just as the Germans were first called Germans by the Celts.

2. *A distinct dialect, peculiar to this tribe alone.* Tribe and

dialect are substantially coextensive; the formation through segmentation of new tribes and dialects was still proceeding in America until quite recently, and most probably has not entirely stopped even today. When two weakened tribes have merged into one, the exceptional case occurs of two closely related dialects being spoken in the same tribe. The average strength of American tribes is under 2,000 members; the Cherokees, however, number about 26,000, the greatest number of Indians in the United States speaking the same dialect.

3. *The right to install into office the sachems and war chiefs elected by the gentes and the right to depose them*, even against the will of their gens. As these sachems and war chiefs are members of the council of the tribe, these rights of the tribe in regard to them explain themselves. Where a confederacy of tribes had been formed with all the tribes represented in a federal council, these rights were transferred to the latter.

4. *The possession of common religious conceptions (mythology) and ceremonies.* 'After the fashion of barbarians the American Indians were a religious people' [Morgan, p. 117]. Their mythology has not yet been studied at all critically. They already embodied their religious ideas – spirits of every kind – in human form; but the lower stage of barbarism which they had reached still knows no plastic representations, so-called idols. Their religion is a cult of nature and of elemental forces in process of development to polytheism. The various tribes had their regular festivals with definite rites, especially dances and games. Dancing particularly was an essential part of all religious ceremonies; each tribe held its own celebration separately.

5. *A tribal council for the common affairs of the tribe.* It was composed of all the sachems and war chiefs of the different gentes, who were genuinely representative because they could be deposed at any time. It held its deliberations in public surrounded by the other members of the tribe, who had the right to join freely in the discussion and to make their views heard. The decision rested with the council. As a rule, everyone was given a hearing who asked for it; the

women could also have their views expressed by a speaker of their own choice. Among the Iroquois the final decision had to be unanimous, as was also the case in regard to many decisions of the German mark communities. The tribal council was responsible especially for the handling of relations with other tribes; it received and sent embassies, declared war and made peace. If war broke out, it was generally carried on by volunteers. In principle, every tribe was considered to be in a state of war with every other tribe with which it had not expressly concluded a treaty of peace. Military expeditions against such enemies were generally organized by prominent individual warriors; they held a war dance, and whoever joined in the dance announced thereby his participation in the expedition. The column was at once formed and started off. The defence of the tribal territory when attacked was also generally carried out by volunteers. The departure and return of such columns were always an occasion of public festivities. The consent of the tribal council was not required for such expeditions, and was neither asked nor given. They find their exact counterpart in the private war expeditions of the German retinues described by Tacitus, only with the difference that among the Germans the retinues have already acquired a more permanent character forming a firm core already organized in peacetime to which the other volunteers are attached in event of war. These war parties are seldom large; the most important expeditions of the Indians, even to great distances, were undertaken with insignificant forces. If several such parties united for operations on a large scale, each was under the orders only of its own leader. Unity in the plan of campaign was secured well or ill by a council of these leaders. It is the same manner of warfare as we find described by Ammianus Marcellinus among the Alemanni on the Upper Rhine in the fourth century.

6. *Among some tribes we find a head chief whose powers, however, are very slight.* He is one of the sachems, and in situations demanding swift action he has to take provisional measures until the council can assemble and make a definite decision. His function represents the first feeble attempt at the creation

of an official with executive power, though generally nothing more came of it; as we shall see, the executive official developed in most cases, if not in all, out of the chief military commander.

The great majority of the American Indians did not advance to any higher form of association than the tribe. Living in small tribes, separated from one another by wide tracts between their frontiers, weakened by incessant wars, they occupied an immense territory with few people. Here and there alliances between related tribes came into being in the emergency of the moment and broke up when the emergency had passed. But in certain districts tribes which were originally related and had then been dispersed joined together again in permanent federations, thus taking the first step toward the formation of nations. In the United States we find the most developed form of such a federation among the Iroquois. Emigrating from their homes west of the Mississippi where they probably formed a branch of the great Dakota family, they settled after long wanderings in what is now the State of New York. They were divided into five tribes: Senecas, Cayugas, Onondagas, Oneidas and Mohawks. They subsisted on fish, game and the products of a crude horticulture, and lived in villages which were generally protected by a stockade. Never more than 20,000 strong, they had a number of gentes common to all the five tribes, spoke closely related dialects of the same language, and occupied a continuous stretch of territory which was divided up among the five tribes. As they had newly conquered this territory, these tribes were naturally accustomed to stand together against the inhabitants they had driven out. From this developed at the beginning of the fifteenth century at latest a regular 'everlasting league', a sworn confederacy, which in the consciousness of its new strength immediately assumed an aggressive character and at the height of its power, about 1675, conquered wide stretches of the surrounding country, either expelling the inhabitants or making them pay tribute. The Iroquois confederacy represents the most advanced social organization achieved by any Indians still at the lower stage

126

of barbarism (excluding, therefore, the Mexicans, New Mexicans and Peruvians).

The main provisions of the confederacy were as follows:

1. Perpetual federation of the five consanguineous tribes on the basis of complete equality and independence in all internal matters of the tribe. This bond of kin represented the real basis of the confederacy. Of the five tribes, three were known as father tribes and were brother tribes to one another; the other two were known as son tribes and were likewise brother tribes to one another. Three gentes, the oldest, still had their living representatives in all five tribes, and another three in three tribes; the members of each of these gentes were all brothers of one another throughout all the five tribes. Their common language, in which there were only variations of dialect, was the expression and the proof of their common descent.

2. The organ of the confederacy was a federal council of fifty sachems, all equal in rank and authority; the decisions of this council were final in all matters relating to the confederacy.

3. The fifty sachems were distributed among the tribes and gentes at the foundation of the confederacy to hold the new offices specially created for federal purposes. They were elected by the respective gentes whenever a vacancy occurred and could be deposed by the gentes at any time; but the right of investing them with their office belonged to the federal council.

4. These federal sachems were also sachems in their respective tribes, and had a seat and a vote in the tribal council.

5. All decisions of the federal council had to be unanimous.

6. Voting was by tribes, so that for a decision to be valid every tribe and all members of the council in every tribe had to signify their agreement.

7. Each of the five tribal councils could convene the federal council, but it could not convene itself.

8. The meetings of the council were held in the presence of the assembled people; every Iroquois could speak; the council alone decided.

9. The confederacy had no official head or chief executive officer.

10. On the other hand, the council had two principal war chiefs, with equal powers and equal authority (the two 'kings' of the Spartans, the two consuls in Rome).

That was the whole public constitution under which the Iroquois lived for over 400 years and are still living today. I have described it fully, following Morgan, because here we have the opportunity of studying the organization of society which still has no *state*. The state presupposes a special public power separated from the body of the people, and Maurer, who with a true instinct recognizes that the constitution of the German mark is a purely social institution differing essentially from the state though later providing a great part of its basis, consequently investigates in all his writings the gradual growth of the public power out of and side by side with the primitive constitutions of marks, villages, homesteads, and towns. Among the North American Indians we see how an originally homogeneous tribe gradually spreads over a huge continent; how through division tribes become nations, entire groups of tribes; how the languages change until they not only become unintelligible to other tribes but also lose almost every trace of their original identity; how at the same time within the tribes each gens splits up into several gentes, how the old mother gentes are preserved as phratries, while the names of these oldest gentes nevertheless remain the same in widely distant tribes that have long been separated – the Wolf and the Bear are still gentile names among a majority of all Indian tribes. And the constitution described above applies in the main to them all, except that many of them never advanced as far as the confederacy of related tribes.

But once the gens is given as the social unit we also see how the whole constitution of gentes, phratries, and tribes is almost necessarily bound to develop from this unit, because the development is natural. Gens, phratry, and tribe are all groups of different degrees of consanguinity, each self-contained and ordering its own affairs, but each supplementing the other. And the affairs which fall within their sphere comprise all the public affairs of barbarians of the lower stage. When we find a people with the gens as their social unit, we may therefore also look for an organization of the tribe similar to that here described; and when there are adequate sources as in the case of the Greeks and the Romans, we shall not find it, but we shall also be able to convince ourselves that where the sources fail us comparison with the American social constitution helps us over the most difficult doubts and riddles.

And a wonderful constitution it is, this gentile constitution, in all its childlike simplicity! No soldiers, no gendarmes or police, no nobles, kings, regents, prefects, or judges, no prisons, or lawsuits – and everything takes its orderly course. All quarrels and disputes are settled by the whole of the community affected, by the gens or the tribe, or by the gentes among themselves; only as an extreme and exceptional measure is blood revenge threatened – and our capital punishment is nothing but blood revenge in a civilized form, with all the advantages and drawbacks of civilization. Although there were many more matters to be settled in common than today – the household is maintained by a number of families in common and is communistic; the land belongs to the tribe, only the small gardens are allotted provisionally to the households – yet there is no need for even a trace of our complicated administrative apparatus with all its ramifications. The decisions are taken by those concerned, and in most cases everything has been already settled by the custom of centuries. There cannot be any poor or needy – the communal household and the gens know their responsibilities toward the old, the sick, and those disabled in war. All are equal and free – the women included. There is no place yet for slaves, nor, as a rule, for the subjugation of other tribes. When about the year 1651 the Iroquois had conquered the Eries and the 'Neutral Nation', they offered to accept them into the confederacy on equal terms; it was only after the defeated tribes had refused that they were driven from their territory. And what men and women such a society breeds is proved by the admiration inspired in all white people who have come into contact with unspoiled Indians, by the personal dignity, uprightness, strength of character, and courage of these barbarians.

We have seen examples of this courage quite recently in Africa. The Zulus a few years ago and the Nubians a few months ago – both of them tribes in which gentile institutions have not yet died out – did what no European army can do. Armed only with lances and spears, without firearms, under a hail of bullets from the breechloaders of the English infantry – acknowledged the best in the world at fighting in close order – they advanced right up to the bayonets and more than once threw the lines into disorder and even broke them, in spite of the enormous inequality of weapons and in spite of the fact that they have no military service and know nothing of drill. Their powers of endurance and performance are shown by the complaint of the English that a Kaffir travels farther and faster in 24 hours than a horse. His smallest muscle stands out hard and firm like whipcord, says an English painter.

That is what men and society were before the division into classes. And when we compare their position with that of the overwhelming majority of civilized men today, an enormous gulf separates the present-day proletarian and small peasant from the free member of the old gentile society.

That is the one side. But we must not forget that this organization was doomed. It did not go beyond the tribe. The confederacy of tribes already marks the beginning of its collapse, as we shall see later, and was already apparent in the attempts at subjugation by the Iroquois. Outside the tribe was outside the law. Wherever there was not an explicit treaty of peace, tribe was at war with tribe, and wars were waged with the cruelty which distinguishes man from other animals and which was only mitigated later by self-interest. The gentile constitution in its best days, as we saw it in America, presupposed an extremely undeveloped state of production and therefore an extremely sparse population over a wide area. Man's attitude to nature was therefore one of almost complete subjection to a strange incomprehensible power, as is reflected in his childish religious conceptions. Man was bounded by his tribe, both in relation to strangers from outside the tribe and to himself; the tribe, the gens, and their institutions were sacred and inviolable, a higher power established by nature to which the individual subjected himself unconditionally in feeling, thought, and action. However impressive the people of this epoch appear to us, they are completely undifferentiated from one another; as Marx says, they are still attached to the navel string of the primitive community.[6] The power of this primitive community had to be broken, and it was broken. But it was broken by influences which from the very start appear as a degradation, a fall from the simple moral greatness of the old gentile society. The lowest interests – base greed, brutal appetites, sordid avarice, selfish robbery of the common wealth – inaugurate the new, civilized, class society. It is by the vilest means – theft, violence, fraud, treason – that the old classless gentile society is undermined and overthrown. And the new society itself during all the 2,500 years of its existence has never been anything else but the development of the small minority at the expense of the great exploited and oppressed majority; today it is so more than ever before.

6. See *Capital*, Vol. 1 (Penguin, 1976), pp. 172–3.

CHAPTER IV

The Greek Gens

From prehistoric times Greeks and Pelasgians alike, and other peoples of kindred stock, had been organized in the same organic series as the Americans: gens, phratry, tribe, confederacy of tribes. The phratry might be absent, as among the Dorians, and the confederacy of tribes was not necessarily fully developed everywhere as yet; but in every case the gens was the unit. At the time of their entry into history, the Greeks are on the threshold of civilization; between them and the American tribes, of whom we spoke above, lie almost two entire great periods of development by which the Greeks of the heroic age are ahead of the Iroquois. The gens of the Greeks is therefore no longer the archaic gens of the Iroquois; the impress of group marriage is beginning to be a good deal blurred. Mother right has given way to father right; increasing private wealth has thus made its first breach in the gentile constitution. A second breach followed naturally from the first. After the introduction of father right, the property of a rich heiress would have passed to her husband and thus into another gens on her marriage, but the foundation of all gentile law was now violated and in such a case the girl was not only permitted but *ordered* to marry within the gens, in order that her property should be retained for the gens.

According to Grote's *A History of Greece* [1869; III, pp. 54–5], the Athenian gens in particular was held together by the following institutions and customs:

1. Common religious rites and the exclusive privilege of priesthood in honour of a particular god, the supposed

ancestral father of the gens, who in this attribute was designated by a special surname.

2. A common burial place (*see* Demosthenes' *Eubulides*).

3. Mutual right of inheritance.

4. Mutual obligations of help, protection, and assistance in case of violence.

5. Mutual right and obligation to marry within the gens in certain cases, especially for orphan girls and heiresses.

6. Possession, at least in some cases, of common property with a special archon (chief magistrate) and treasurer.

Next, several gentes were united in the phratry, but less closely; though here also we find mutual rights and obligations of a similar kind, particularly the common celebration of certain religious ceremonies and the right to avenge the death of a phrator. Similarly, all the phratries of a tribe held regularly recurring religious festivals in common at which a leader of the tribe (*phylobasileus*), elected from the nobility (*eupatrida*), officiated.

Thus Grote, and Marx adds: 'In the Greek gens, the savage (for example, Iroquois) shows through unmistakably.' He becomes still more unmistakable when we investigate further.

For the Greek gens has also the following characteristics:

7. Descent in the male line.

8. Prohibition of marriage within the gens except in the case of heiresses. This exception and its formulation as an ordinance prove the old rule to be valid. This is further substantiated by the universally accepted principle that at her marriage the woman renounced the religious rites of her gens, and went over to those of her husband, being also inscribed in his phratry. This custom and a famous passage in Dicaearchus both show that marriage outside the gens was the rule, and Becker in *Charicles* directly assumes that nobody might marry within his own gens.

9. The right of adoption into the gens. This was exercised through adoption into the family but required public formalities and was exceptional.

10. The right to elect chieftains and to depose them. We know that every gens had its archon; but it is nowhere stated

that the office was hereditary in certain families. Until the end of barbarism the probability is always against strict heredity, which is quite incompatible with conditions in which rich and poor had completely equal rights within the gens.

Not only Grote but also Niebuhr, Mommsen and all the other historians of classical antiquity have come to grief over the gens. Though they correctly noted many of its character-istics, they always took it to be a *group of families*, thus making it impossible for themselves to understand the nature and origin of the gens. Under the gentile constitution, the family was never an organizational unit and could not be so, for man and wife necessarily belonged to two different gentes. The whole gens was incorporated within the phratry and the whole phratry within the tribe; but the family belonged half to the gens of the man and half to the gens of the woman. In public law the state also does not recognize the family; up to this day, the family only exists for private law. And yet all our histories have hitherto started from the absurd assump-tion, which since the eighteenth century in particular has become inviolable, that the monogamous single family, which is hardly older than civilization, is the core around which society and state have gradually crystallized.

Mr Grote will also please note [Marx throws in] that though the Greeks derive their gentes from mythology, the gentes are older than the mythology which *they themselves* created with all its gods and demigods.

Morgan prefers to quote Grote because he is not only an impressive but also a trustworthy witness. Grote goes on to say that every Athenian gens had a name derived from its supposed ancestor; that it was the general custom before Solon, and even after Solon, in the absence of a will for the property of a deceased person to pass to the members of his gens (*gennêtes*); and that in the case of a murder it was the right and the duty, first of the relatives of the murdered man, then of the members of his gens, and lastly of his phratry, to prosecute the criminal before the tribunals: 'All that we hear of the most ancient Athenian laws is based upon the gentile and phratric divisions' [Grote, III, p. 66].

The descent of the gentes from common ancestors has caused the 'pedantic philistines', as Marx calls them, a lot of brain-racking. As they of course declare the common ancestors to be pure myths, they are at an utter loss to explain how the gens originated out of a number of separate and originally quite unrelated families; yet they have to perform this feat in order to explain how the gentes exist at all. So they argue in a whirlpool of words, never getting any further than the statement: the ancestral tree is a fairy tale, but the gens is a reality. And finally Grote declares (interpolations by Marx):

We hear of this genealogy but rarely because it is only brought before the public in certain cases pre-eminent and venerable. But the humbler gentes had their common rites [this is strange, Mr Grote!], and common superhuman ancestor and genealogy, as well as the more celebrated [this is most strange, Mr Grote, among *humbler* gentes!]: the scheme and ideal basis [my good sir, not *ideal*, but carnal, *germanic fleishlich*!] was the same in all [Grote, III, p. 60].

Marx summarizes Morgan's reply to this as follows:

The system of consanguinity corresponding to the original form of the gens – and the Greeks like other mortals once possessed such a gens – preserved the knowledge of the mutual relations between all the members of the gens. It was of decisive importance for them, and they learned it by practice from childhood upwards. With the monogamous family, this knowledge was forgotten. The gentile name created an ancestral tree, beside which that of the individual family appeared insignificant. It was now the function of this name to preserve the fact of the common descent of those who bore it; but the lineage of the gens went back so far that its members could not prove the actual relationship existing between them, except in a limited number of cases through more recent common ancestors. The name itself was proof of common descent and conclusive proof, apart from cases of adoption. Actually to deny, like Grote and Niebuhr, all relationship between the members of the gens, thus changing the gens into a purely fictitious and imaginary creation, is worthy of 'ideal', that is, pedantic bookworms. Because the ties of kinship, especially with the rise of monogamy, are pushed back into remote times and the reality of the past appears reflected in mythological phantasies, our good philistines concluded, and conclude, that the imaginary pedigree created the real gentes!

The phratry, as among the Americans, was a mother gens that had split up into several daughter gentes and now united them; often it still traced all the gentes back to its own common ancestral father. According to Grote, 'all the contemporary members of the phratry of Hekataeus had a common god for their ancestor at the sixteenth degree' [Grote, II, pp. 58–9]; all gentes of this phratry were therefore literally brother gentes. The phratry still appears in Homer as a military unit in the famous passage where Nestor advises Agamemnon: 'Marshal the men by tribes and by phratries, so that phratry may assist phratry and tribe may assist tribe.'

The phratry has further the right and the duty of prosecuting for bloodguilt incurred against a phrator; hence in earlier times it also had the obligation of blood revenge. Further, it had common shrines and festivals; in fact the elaboration of the whole Greek mythology out of the traditional old Aryan nature cult was essentially conditioned by the phratries and gentes and took place within them. The phratry also had a chief (the *phratriarchos*) and, according to de Coulanges, assemblies which could pass binding resolutions, a tribunal and an administration. Even the later state, while it ignored the gens, left certain public offices in the hands of the phratry.

Several related phratries form a tribe. In Attica there were four tribes, each consisting of three phratries, each phratry numbering thirty gentes. Such a rounded symmetry of groups presupposes conscious, purposeful interference with the naturally developed order. As to how, when, and why this occurred, Greek history is silent; the historical memory of the Greeks only went back to the heroic age.

As the Greeks were crowded together in a relatively small territory, differences of dialect were less developed than in the wide American forests; yet in Greece also it was only tribes of the same main dialect that united in a larger organization, and even Attica, small as it was, had a dialect of its own, which later through its general use as the language of prose became the dominant dialect.

In the Homeric poems we find most of the Greek tribes already united into small nations, within which, however, gentes, phratries, and tribes retained their full independence. They already lived in towns fortified with walls; the population increased with the increase of the herds, the extension of agriculture and the beginnings of handicraft. The differences in wealth thus became more pronounced and with them the aristocratic element within the old primitive democracy. The various small nations waged incessant wars for the possession of the best land and doubtless also for booty; the use of prisoners of war as slaves was already a recognized institution.

The constitution of these tribes and small nations was as follows:

1. The permanent authority was the council (*boulè*), probably composed originally of all the chiefs of the gentes, but later, when their number became too large, of a selection whose choice provided an opportunity of extending and strengthening the aristocratic element. Dionysius actually speaks of the council in the heroic age as composed of nobles (*kratistoi*). The ultimate decision in important matters rested with the council. Thus in Aeschylus [*Seven Against Thebes*] the council of Thebes makes what is in the circumstances the vital decision to give Eteocles an honourable burial, but to throw out the corpse of Polynices to be devoured by dogs. When the state was established, this council was merged into the senate.

2. The assembly of the people (*agora*). We saw among the Iroquois how the people, men and women, stood round the council when it was holding its meetings, intervening in an orderly manner in its deliberations and thus influencing its decisions. Among the Homeric Greeks, this *Umstand* [those standing round], to use an old German legal expression, had already developed into a regular assembly of the people, as was also the case among the Germans in primitive times. It

was convened by the council to decide important questions; every man had the right to speak. The decision was given by a show of hands (Aeschylus, *The Suppliants*) or by acclamation. The decision of the assembly was supreme and final, for, says Schömann, in *Griechische Altertümer* [Antiquities of Greece] 'if the matter was one requiring the cooperation of the people for its execution, Homer does not indicate any means by which the people could be forced to cooperate against their will'.

For at this time, when every adult male member of the tribe was a warrior, there was as yet no public power separate from the people which could have been used against the people. Primitive democracy was still in its full strength, and it is in relation to that fact that the power and the position both of the council and of the *basileus* must first be judged.

3. The leader of the army (*basileus*). Marx makes the following comment:

European scholars, born lackeys most of them, make the *basileus* into a monarch in the modern sense. Morgan, the Yankee republican, protests. Very ironically, but truly, he says of the oily-tongued Gladstone and his *Juventus Mundi*: 'Mr Gladstone, who presents to his readers the Grecian chiefs of the heroic age as kings and princes, with the superadded qualities of gentlemen, is forced to admit that "on the whole we seem to have the custom or law of primogeniture sufficiently but not oversharply defined" ' [Morgan, p. 225n.].

Mr Gladstone will probably agree that such an ambiguous law of primogeniture as may be 'sufficiently but not oversharply defined' is just as good as none at all.

In what sense the offices of sachem and chieftain were hereditary among the Iroquois and other Indians we have already seen. All offices were elective, generally within a gens, and to that extent hereditary to the gens. In the course of time, preference when filling vacancies was given to the nearest gentile relation – brother or sister's son – unless there were reasons for passing him over. The fact that among the Greeks under father right the office of *basileus* generally passed to the son or one of the sons only proves that the probabilities were in favour of the sons succeeding to the office by popular election; it is no proof at all of legal hereditary succession without popular election. All that we have here is the first beginnings among the Iroquois and Greeks of distinct noble families within the gentes and, in the case of the Greeks, the first beginnings also of a future hereditary leadership or monarchy. The probability is, therefore, that among the Greeks the *basileus* had either to be elected by the people or at least confirmed in his office by the recognized organs of the people, the council or *agora*, as was the case with the Roman 'king' (*rex*).

In the *Iliad* Agamemnon, the ruler of men, does not appear as the supreme king of the Greeks, but as supreme commander of a federal army before a besieged town. It is to this supremacy of command that Odysseus, after disputes had broken out among the Greeks, refers in a famous passage: 'Evil is the rule of many; let one be commander,' etc. (The favourite line about the sceptre is a later addition.)

Odysseus is here not giving a lecture on a form of government, but demanding obedience to the supreme commander in war. Since they are appearing before Troy only as an army, the proceedings in the *agora* secure to the Greeks all necessary democracy. When Achilles speaks of presents – that is, the division of the booty – he always leaves the division, not to Agamemnon or any other *basileus*, but to the 'sons of the Achaeans', that is, the people. Such epithets as 'descended from Zeus', 'nourished by Zeus', prove nothing, for *every* gens is descended from a god, that of the leader of the tribe being already descended from a 'superior' god, in this case Zeus. Even those without personal freedom, such as the swineherd Eumaeus and others, are 'divine' (*dioi* and *theioi*), and that too in the *Odyssey* which is much later than the *Iliad*; and again in the *Odyssey* the name *Heros* is given to the herald Mulios as well as to the blind bard Demodocus. Since, in short, council and assembly of the people function together with the *basileus*, the word *basileia*, which Greek writers employ to denote the so-called Homeric kinship (chief command in the army being the principal characteristic of the office), only means – military democracy (Marx).

In addition to his military functions, the *basileus* also held those of priest and judge, the latter not clearly defined, the former exercised in his capacity as supreme representative of the tribe or confederacy of tribes. There is never any mention of civil administrative powers; he seems, however, to be a member of the council *ex officio*. It is therefore quite correct etymologically to translate *basileus* as king since king (*kuning*) is derived from *kuni*, *künne*, and means head of a gens. But the old Greek *basileus* does not correspond in any way to the present meaning of the word 'king'. Thucydides expressly refers to the old *basileia* as *patrike*, that is, derived from gentes, and says it had strictly defined and therefore limited functions. And Aristotle says that the *basileia* of the heroic age was a leadership over freemen and that the *basileus* was military leader, judge and high priest; he thus had no governmental power in the later sense. *

Thus in the Greek constitution of the heroic age, we see the old gentile order as still a living force. But we also see the beginnings of its disintegration: father right, with transmission of the property to the children by which accumulation of wealth within the family was favoured and the family itself became a power against the gens; reaction of the inequality of wealth on the constitution by the formation of the first rudiments of hereditary nobility and monarchy; slavery, at first only of prisoners of war but already preparing the way for the enslavement of fellow members of the tribe and even of the gens; the old wars between tribe and tribe already degenerating into systematic pillage by land and sea for the acquisition of cattle, slaves and treasure, and becoming a regular source of wealth; in short, riches praised and

* Like the Greek *basileus*, so also the Aztec military chief has been made out to be a modern prince. The report of the Spaniards, which were at first misinterpretations and exaggerations, and later actual lies, were submitted for the first time to historical criticism by Morgan. He proves that the Mexicans were at the middle stage of barbarism, though more advanced than the New Mexican Pueblo Indians, and that their constitution, so far as it can be recognized in the distorted reports, corresponded to this stage: a confederacy of three tribes which had subjugated a number of other tribes and exacted tribute from them, and which was governed by a federal council and a federal military leader, out of whom the Spaniards made an 'emperor'.

respected as the highest good and the old gentile order misused to justify the violent seizure of riches. Only one thing was wanting: an institution which not only secured the newly acquired riches of individuals against the communistic traditions of the gentile order, which not only sanctified the private property formerly so little valued and declared this sanctification to be the highest purpose of all human society; but, an institution which set the seal of general social recognition on each new method of acquiring property and thus amassing wealth at continually increasing speed; an institution which perpetuated not only this growing cleavage of society into classes but also the right of the possessing class to exploit the non-possessing, and the rule of the former over the latter.

And this institution came. The *state* was invented.

CHAPTER V

The Rise of the Athenian State

How the state developed, how the organs of the gentile constitution were partly transformed in this development, partly pushed aside by the introduction of new organs, and at last superseded entirely by real state authorities while the true 'people in arms', organized for its self-defence in its gentes, phratries and tribes, was replaced by an armed 'public force' in the service of these state authorities and therefore at their command for use also against the people – this process, at least in its first stages, can be followed nowhere better than in ancient Athens. The changes in form have been outlined by Morgan, but their economic content and cause must largely be added by myself.

In the heroic age the four tribes of the Athenians were still settled in Attica in separate territories; even the twelve phratries composing them seem still to have had distinct seats in the twelve towns of Cecrops. The constitution was that of the heroic age: assembly of the people, council of the people, a *basileus*. As far back as written history goes, we find the land already divided up and privately owned, which is in accordance with the relatively advanced commodity production and the corresponding trade in commodities developed toward the end of the upper stage of barbarism. In addition to grain, wine and oil were produced; to a continually increasing extent, the sea trade in the Aegean was captured from the Phoenicians, and most of it passed into Athenian hands. Through the sale and purchase of land and the progressive division of labour between agriculture and handicraft, trade, and shipping, it was inevitable that the members of the different gentes, phratries, and tribes very soon became intermixed. Into the districts of the phratry and tribe moved inhabitants, who, although fellow countrymen, did not belong to these bodies and were therefore strangers in their own place of domicile. For when times were quiet, each tribe and each phratry administered its own affairs without sending to Athens to consult the council of the people or the *basileus*. But anyone not a member of the phratry or tribe was, of course, excluded from taking any part in this administration, even though living in the district.

The smooth functioning of the organs of the gentile constitution was thus thrown so much out of gear that even in the heroic age remedies had to be found. The constitution ascribed to Theseus was introduced. The principal change which it made was to set up a central authority in Athens – that is, part of the affairs hitherto administered by the tribes independently were declared common affairs and entrusted to the common council sitting in Athens. In taking this step, the Athenians went further than any native people of America had ever done: instead of neighbouring tribes forming a simple confederacy, they fused together into one single nation. Hence arose a common Athenian civil law which stood above the legal customs of the tribes and gentes. The Athenian citizen as such acquired definite rights and new protection in law even on territory which was not that of his tribe. The first step had been taken toward undermining the gentile constitution; for this was the first step to the later admission of citizens who did not belong to any tribe in all Attica, but were and remained completely outside the Athenian gentile constitution. By a second measure ascribed to Theseus, the entire people, regardless of gens, phratry or tribe, was divided into three classes: *eupatrides* or nobles, *geomoroi* or farmers, and *demiourgoi* or artisans, and the right to hold office was vested exclusively in the nobility. Apart from the tenure of offices by the nobility, this division remained inoperative, as it did not create any other legal distinctions between the classes. It is, however, important because it reveals the new social elements which had been

143

developing unobserved. It shows that the customary appointment of members of certain families to the offices of the gens had already grown into an almost uncontested right of these families to office; it shows that these families, already powerful through their wealth, were beginning to form groupings outside their gentes as a separate, privileged class, and that the state now taking form sanctioned this presumption. It shows further that the division of labour between peasants and artisans was now firmly enough established in its social importance to challenge the old grouping of gentes and tribes. And, finally, it proclaims the irreconcilable opposition between gentile society and the state; the first attempt at forming a state consists in breaking up the gentes by dividing their members into those with privileges and those with none, and by further separating the latter into two productive classes and thus setting them one against the other.

The further political history of Athens up to the time of Solon is only imperfectly known. The office of *basileus* fell into disuse; the positions at the head of the state were occupied by archons elected from the nobility. The power of the nobility continuously increased until about the year 600 BC it became insupportable. And the principal means for suppressing the common liberty were – money and usury. The nobility had their chief seat in and around Athens, whose maritime trade, with occasional piracy still thrown in, enriched them and concentrated in their hands the wealth existing in the form of money. From here the growing money economy penetrated like corrosive acid into the old traditional life of the rural communities founded on natural economy. The gentile constitution is absolutely irreconcilable with money economy; the ruin of the Attic small farmers coincided with the loosening of the old gentile bonds which embraced and protected them. The debtor's bond and the lien on property (for already the Athenians had invented the mortgage also) respected neither gens nor phratry, while the old gentile constitution for its part knew neither money nor advances of money nor debts in money. Hence the money rule of the aristocracy now in full flood of expansion also

144

created a new customary law to secure the creditor against the debtor and to sanction the exploitation of the small peasant by the possessor of money. All the fields of Attica were thick with mortgage columns bearing inscriptions stating that the land on which they stood was mortgaged to such and such for so and so much. The fields not so marked had for the most part already been sold on account of unpaid mortgages or interest and had passed into the ownership of the noble usurer. The peasant could count himself lucky if he was allowed to remain on the land as a tenant and live on *one sixth* of the produce of his labour while he paid *five sixths* to his new master as rent. And that was not all. If the sale of the land did not cover the debt or if the debt had been contracted without any security, the debtor, in order to meet his creditor's claims, had to sell his children into slavery abroad. Children sold by their father – such was the first fruit of father right and monogamy! And if the bloodsucker was still not satisfied, he could sell the debtor himself as a slave. Thus the pleasant dawn of civilization began for the Athenian people.

Formerly, when the conditions of the people still corresponded to the gentile constitution, such an upheaval was impossible; now it had happened – nobody knew how. Let us go back for a moment to the Iroquois, amongst whom the situation now confronting the Athenians, without their own doing so to speak and certainly against their will, was inconceivable. Their mode of producing the necessities of life, unvarying from year to year, could never generate such conflicts as were apparently forced on the Athenians from without; it could never create an opposition of rich and poor, of exploiters and exploited. The Iroquois were still very far from controlling nature, but within the limits imposed on them by natural forces they did control their own production. Apart from bad harvests in their small gardens, the exhaustion of the stocks of fish in their lakes and rivers or of the game in their woods, they knew what results they could expect making their living as they did. The certain result was a livelihood, plentiful or scanty; but one result there could never be – social upheavals that no one had ever intended, sundering of the gentile bonds, division of gens and tribe into two opposing and warring classes. Production was limited in the extreme, but – the producers controlled their product. That was the immense advantage of barbarian production which was lost with the coming of civilization; to reconquer it, but on the basis of the gigantic control of nature now achieved by man and of the free association now made possible, will be the task of the next generations.

Not so among the Greeks. The rise of private property in herds and articles of luxury led to exchange between individuals, to the transformation of products into *commodities*. And here lie the seeds of the whole subsequent upheaval. When the producers no longer directly consumed their product themselves, but let it pass out of their hands in the act of exchange, they lost control of it. They no longer knew what became of it; the possibility was there that one day it would be used against the producer to exploit and oppress him. For this reason no society can permanently retain the mastery of its own production and the control over the social effects of its process of production unless it abolishes exchange between individuals.

But the Athenians were soon to learn how rapidly the product asserts its mastery over the producer when once exchange between individuals has begun and products have been transformed into commodities. With the coming of commodity production, individuals began to cultivate the soil on their own account, which soon led to individual ownership of land. Money followed, the general commodity with which all others were exchangeable. But when men invented money, they did not think that they were again creating a new social power, the one general power before which the whole of society must bow. And it was this new power, suddenly sprung to life without knowledge or will of its creators, which now in all the brutality of its youth gave the Athenians the first taste of its might.

What was to be done? The old gentile constitution had not only shown itself powerless before the triumphal march of money; it was absolutely incapable of finding any place within its framework for such things as money, creditors, debtors, and forcible collection of debts. But the new social power was there; pious wishes, and yearning for the return of the good old days would not drive money and usury out of the world. Further, a number of minor breaches had also been made in the gentile constitution. All over Attica, and especially in Athens itself, the members of the different gentes and phratries became still more indiscriminately mixed with every generation although even now an Athenian was only allowed to sell land outside his gens, not the house in which he lived. The division of labour between the different branches of production – agriculture, handicrafts (in which there were again innumerable subdivisions), shipping, and so forth – had been carried further with every advance of industry and commerce. The population was now divided according to occupation into fairly permanent groups, each with its new common interests; and since the gens and the phratry made no provision for dealing with them, new offices had to be created. The number of slaves had increased considerably and even at that time must have far exceeded the number of free Athenians. The gentile constitution originally knew nothing of slavery and therefore had no means of keeping these masses of bondsmen in order. Finally, trade had brought to Athens a number of foreigners who settled there on account of the greater facilities of making money; they also could claim no rights or protection under the old constitution; and, though they were received with traditional tolerance, they remained a disturbing and alien body among the people.

In short, the end of the gentile constitution was approaching. Society was outgrowing it more every day; even the worst evils that had grown up under its eyes were beyond its power to check or remove. But in the meantime the state had quietly been developing. The new groups formed by the division of labour, first between town and country, then between the different branches of town labour, had created new organs to look after their interests; official posts of all kinds had been set up. And above everything else the young state needed a power of its own, which in the case of the seafaring Athenians could at first only be a naval power, for the purpose of carrying on occasional small wars and protecting its merchant ships. At some unknown date before Solon, the *naukrariai* were set up, small territorial districts, twelve to each tribe; each *naukraria* had to provide, equip and man a warship and also contribute two horsemen. This institution was a twofold attack on the gentile constitution. In the first place, it created a public force which was now no longer simply identical with the whole body of the armed people; secondly, for the first time it divided the people for public purposes, not by groups of kinship, but *by common place of residence*. We shall see the significance of this.

The gentile constitution being incapable of bringing help to the exploited people, there remained only the growing state. And the state brought them its help in the form of the constitution of Solon, thereby strengthening itself again at the expense of the old constitution. Solon – the manner in which his reform, which belongs to the year 594 BC, was carried through does not concern us here – opened the series of so-called political revolutions; and he did so with an attack on property. All revolutions hitherto have been revolutions to protect one kind of property against another kind of property. They cannot protect the one without violating the other. In the great French Revolution feudal property was sacrificed to save bourgeois property; in that of Solon, the property of the creditors had to suffer for the benefit of the property of the debtors. The debts were simply declared void. We do not know the exact details, but in his poems Solon boasts of having removed the mortgage columns from the fields and brought back all the people who had fled or been sold abroad on account of debt. This was only possible by open violation of property. And, in fact, from the first to the last, all so-called political revolutions have been made to protect property – of *one* kind; and they have been carried out by confiscating, also called stealing, property – of *another* kind. The plain truth is that for 2,500 years it has been possible to preserve private property only by violating property rights.

But now the need was to protect the free Athenians against the return of such slavery. The first step was the introduction of general measures – for example, the prohibition of debt contracts pledging the person of the debtor. Further, in order to place at least some check on the nobles' ravening hunger for the land of the peasants, a maximum limit was fixed for the amount of land that could be owned by one individual. Then changes were made in the constitution, of which the most important for us are the following:

The council was raised to 400 members, 100 for each tribe; here, therefore, the tribe was still taken as basis. But that was the one and only feature of the new state incorporating anything from the old constitution. For all other purposes Solon divided the citizens into four classes according to their property in land and the amount of its yield: 500, 300 and 150 *medimni* of grain (one *medimnus* equals about 1·16 bushels) were the minimum yields for the first three classes; those who owned less land or none at all were placed in the fourth class. All offices could be filled only from the three upper classes and the highest offices only from the first. The fourth class only had the right to speak and vote in the assembly of the people; but it was in this assembly that all officers were elected. Here they had to render their account; here all laws were made; and here the fourth class formed the majority. The privileges of the aristocracy were partially renewed in the form of privileges of wealth, but the people retained the decisive power. Further, the four classes formed the basis of a new military organization. The first two classes provided the cavalry; the third had to serve as heavy infantry; the fourth served either as light infantry without armour or in the fleet, for which they probably received wages.

A completely new element is thus introduced into the constitution: private ownership. According to the size of their property in land, the rights and duties of the citizens of the state are now assessed, and in the same degree to which the classes based on property gain influence, the old groups of blood relationship lose it; the gentile constitution had suffered a new defeat.

However, the assessment of political rights on a property basis was not an institution indispensable to the existence of the state. In spite of the great part it has played in the constitutional history of states, very many states, and precisely those most highly developed, have not required it. In Athens also its role was only temporary; from the time of Aristides all offices were open to every citizen.

During the next 80 years Athenian society gradually shaped the course along which it developed in the following centuries. Usury on the security of mortgaged land, which had been rampant in the period before Solon, had been curbed, as had also the inordinate concentration of property in land. Commerce and handicrafts, including artistic handicrafts which were being increasingly developed on a large scale by the use of slave labour, became the main occupations. Athenians were growing more enlightened. Instead of exploiting their fellow citizens in the old brutal way, they exploited chiefly the slaves and the non-Athenian customers. Movable property, wealth in the form of money, of slaves and ships continually increased, but it was no longer a mere means to the acquisition of landed property as in the old slow days: it had become an end in itself. On the one hand the old power of the aristocracy now had to contend with successful competition from the new class of rich industrialists and merchants; but, on the other hand, the ground was also cut away from beneath the last remains of the old gentile constitution. The gentes, phratries, and tribes whose members were now scattered over all Attica and thoroughly intermixed had thus become useless as political bodies; numbers of Athenian citizens did not belong to any gens at all; they were immigrants who had indeed acquired rights of citizenship, but had not been adopted into any of the old kinship organizations; in addition, there was the steadily increasing number of foreign immigrants who only had rights of protection.

Meanwhile, the fights went on between parties. The nobility tried to win back their former privileges and for a moment regained the upper hand until the revolution of Cleisthenes (509 BC) overthrew them finally, but with them also the last remnants of the gentile constitution.

In his new constitution, Cleisthenes ignored the four old tribes founded on gentes and phratries. In their place appeared a completely new organization on the basis of division of the citizens merely according to their place of residence, such as had been already attempted in the *nau-krariai*. Only domicile was now decisive, not membership of a kinship group. Not the people, but the territory was now divided: the inhabitants became a mere political appendage of the territory.

The whole of Attica was divided into 100 communal districts, called 'demes', each of which was self-governing. The citizens resident in each deme (*demotes*) elected their president (demarch) and treasurer, as well as 30 judges with jurisdiction in minor disputes. They were also given their own temple and patron divinity or hero, whose priests they elected. Supreme power in the deme was vested in the assembly of the *demotes*. As Morgan rightly observes, here is the prototype of the self-governing American township. The modern state in its highest development ends in the same unit with which the rising state in Athens began.

Ten of these units (demes) formed a tribe, which, however, is now known as a local tribe to distinguish it from the old tribe of kinship. The local tribe was not only a self-governing political body, but also a military body; it elected its phylarch, or tribal chief, who commanded the cavalry, the taxiarch commanding the infantry, and the *strategos*, who was in command over all the forces raised in the tribal area. It further provided five warships with their crews and commanders and received as patron deity an Attic hero after whom it was named. Lastly, it elected 50 councillors to the Athenian council.

At the summit was the Athenian state governed by the council composed of the 500 councillors elected by the ten tribes, and in the last instance by the assembly of the people at which every Athenian citizen had the right to attend and to vote; archons and other officials managed the various departments of administration and justice. In Athens there was no supreme official with executive power.

Through this new constitution and the admission to civil rights of a very large number of protected persons, partly immigrants, partly freed slaves, the organs of the gentile constitution were forced out of public affairs; they sank to the level of private associations and religious bodies. But the moral influence of the old gentile period and its traditional ways of thought were still handed down for a long time to come and only died out gradually. We find evidence of this in another state institution.

We saw that an essential characteristic of the state is the existence of a public force differentiated from the mass of the people. At this time, Athens still had only a people's army and a fleet provided directly by the people. Army and fleet gave protection against external enemies and kept in check the slaves, who already formed the great majority of the population. In relation to the citizens, the public power at first existed only in the form of the police force, which is as old as the state itself; for which reason the naive French of the eighteenth century did not speak of civilized peoples but of policed peoples (*nations policées*). The Athenians then instituted a police force simultaneously with their state, a veritable gendarmerie of bowmen, foot and mounted *Land-jäger* [the country's hunters] as they call them in South Germany and Switzerland. But this gendarmerie consisted of *slaves*. The free Athenian considered police duty so degrading that he would rather be arrested by an armed slave than himself have any hand in such despicable work. That was still the old gentile spirit. The state could not exist without police, but the state was still young and could not yet inspire enough moral respect to make honourable an occupation which to the older members of the gens necessarily appeared infamous.

Now complete in its main features, the state was perfectly adapted to the new social conditions of the Athenians as is shown by the rapid growth of wealth, commerce, and industry. The class opposition on which the social and political institutions rested was no longer that of nobility and common people, but of slaves and free men, of protected persons and citizens. At the time of their greatest prosperity, the entire free-citizen population of Athens, women and children included, numbered about 90,000; besides them there were 365,000 slaves of both sexes and 45,000 protected persons – aliens and freedmen. There were therefore at least 18 slaves and more than two protected persons to every adult male citizen. The reason for the large number of slaves was that many of them worked together in manufactories in large rooms under overseers. But with the development of commerce and industry, wealth was accumulated and concentrated in a few hands, and the mass of the free citizens were impoverished. Their only alternatives were to compete against slave labour with their own labour as handicraftsmen, which was considered base and vulgar and also offered very little prospect of success, or to become social scrap. Necessarily, in these circumstances, they did the latter, and as they formed the majority, they thereby brought about the downfall of the whole Athenian state. The downfall of Athens was not caused by democracy as the European lickspittle historians assert to flatter their princes, but by slavery, which banned the labour of free citizens.

The rise of the state among the Athenians is a particularly typical example of the formation of a state; first, the process takes place in a pure form without any interference through use of violent force either from without or from within (the usurpation by Pisistratus left no trace of its short duration); second, it shows a very highly developed form of state, the democratic republic, arising directly out of gentile society; and lastly we are sufficiently acquainted with all the essential details.

CHAPTER VI

The Gens and the State in Rome

According to the legendary account of the foundation of Rome, the first settlement was established by a number of Latin gentes (100, says the legend) who were united in a tribe. These were soon joined by a Sabellian tribe, also said to have numbered 100 gentes, and lastly by a third tribe of mixed elements, again said to have been composed of 100 gentes. The whole account reveals at the first glance that very little was still primitive here except the gens, and that even it was in some cases only an offshoot from a mother gens still existing in its original home. The tribes clearly bear the mark of their artificial composition even though they are generally composed out of related elements and after the pattern of the old tribe, which was not made but grew; it is, however, not an impossibility that the core of each of the three tribes was a genuine old tribe. The intermediate group, the phratry, consisted of ten gentes and was called a *curia*; there were therefore 30 *curiae*.

The Roman gens is recognized to be the same institution as the Greek gens; and since the Greek gens is a further development of the social unit whose original form is found among the American Indians, this of course holds true of the Roman gens also. Here therefore we can be more brief.

The Roman gens, at least in the earliest times of Rome, had the following constitution:

1. Mutual right of inheritance among gentile members; the property remained with the gens. Since father right already prevailed in the Roman gens as in the Greek, descendants in

the female line were excluded. According to the Law of the Twelve Tables, the oldest written Roman law known to us, the children, as natural heirs, had the first title to the estate; in default of children, then the agnates (descendants in the *male* line); in default of agnates, the gentiles. In all cases the property remained within the gens. Here we see gentile custom gradually being penetrated by the new legal provisions springing from increased wealth and monogamy: the original equal right of inheritance of all members of the gens is first restricted in practice to the agnates – probably very early, as already mentioned – finally, to the children and their issue in the male line; in the Twelve Tables this appears, of course, in the reverse order.

2. Possession of a common burial place. On their immigration to Rome from Regilli, the patrician gens of Claudi received a piece of land for their own use and also a common burial place in the town. Even in the time of Augustus, the head of Varus, who had fallen in the battle of the Teutoburg Forest, was brought to Rome and interred in the *gentilitius tumulus* [mound of the gens]; the gens (Quinctilia) therefore still had its own burial mound.

3. Common religious rites. These, the *sacra gentilitia* [sacred celebrations of the gens], are well known.

4. Obligation not to marry within the gens. This seems never to have become written law in Rome, but the custom persisted. Of all the countless Roman married couples whose names have been preserved, there is not one where husband and wife have the same gentile name. The law of inheritance also proves the observance of this rule. The woman loses her agnatic rights on marriage and leaves her gens; neither she nor her children can inherit from her father or his brothers because otherwise the inheritance would be lost to the father's gens. There is no sense in this rule unless a woman may not marry a member of her own gens.

5. Common land. In primitive times the gens had always owned common land ever since the tribal land began to be divided up. Among the Latin tribes, we find the land partly in the possession of the tribe, partly of the gens, and partly

of the households, which at that time can hardly have been single families. Romulus is said to have made the first allotments of land to individuals, about two and one half acres (two *jugera*) to a person. But later we still find land owned by the gentes, to say nothing of the state land, on which the whole internal history of the republic centres.

6. Obligation of mutual protection and help among members of the gens. Only vestiges remain in written history; from the very start the Roman state made its superior power so manifest that the right of protection against injury passed into its hands. When Appius Claudius was arrested, the whole of his gens, even those who were his personal enemies, put on mourning. At the time of the second Punic War [218–201 BC] the gentes joined together to ransom their members who had been taken prisoner; the senate *prohibited* them from doing so.

7. Right to bear the gentile name. This persisted till the time of the emperors; freedmen were allowed to use the gentile name of their former master, but without gentile rights.

8. Right to adopt strangers into the gens. This was done through adoption into a family (as among the Indians), which carried with it acceptance into the gens.

9. The right to elect the chief and to depose him is nowhere mentioned. But since in the earliest days of Rome all offices were filled by election or nomination, from the elected king downward, and since *curiae* also elected their own priests, we may assume the same procedure for the presidents (*principes*) of the gentes – however firmly established the election from one and the same family within the gens may have already become.

Such were the rights of a Roman gens. Apart from the already completed transition to father right, they are the perfect counterpart of the rights and duties in an Iroquois gens; here again 'the Iroquois shows through unmistakably' (Marx).

The confusion that still exists today even among our leading historians on the subject of the Roman gens may be illustrated by one example. In his paper on Roman family names in the period of the Republic and of Augustus (*Römische Forschungen*, Berlin, 1864, I, pp. 8–11) Mommsen writes:

The gentile name belongs to all the male members of the gens, excluding, of course, the slaves, but including adopted and protected persons; it belongs also to the women ... The tribe [as Mommsen here translates *gens*] is ... a communal entity, derived from common lineage (real, supposed or even pretended) and united by communal festivities, burial rites and laws of inheritance; to it all personally free individuals, and therefore all women also, may and must belong. But it is difficult to determine what gentile name was borne by married women. So long as the woman may only marry a member of her own gens, this problem does not arise; and there is evidence that for a long period it was more difficult for women to marry outside than inside the gens; for instance, so late as the sixth century [BC] the right of *gentis enuptio* [marriage outside the gens] was a personal privilege, conceded as a reward ... But when such marriages outside the tribe took place, the wife, in earliest times, must thereby have gone over to her husband's tribe. Nothing is more certain than that the woman, in the old religious marriage, enters completely into the legal and sacramental bonds of her husband's community and leaves her own. Everyone knows that the married woman forfeits the right of inheritance and bequest in relation to members of her own gens but shares rights of inheritance with her husband and children and the members of their gens. And if she is adopted by her husband and taken into his family, how can she remain apart from his gens?

Mommsen therefore maintains that the Roman women who belonged to a gens had originally been permitted to marry only *within* the gens, that the gens had therefore been endogamous, not exogamous. This view, which is in contradiction to all the evidence from other peoples, rests chiefly, if not exclusively, on one much disputed passage from Livy (Book XXXIX, Ch. 19), according to which the senate in the year 568 after the foundation of the city, or 186 BC, decreed: '*Uti Feceniae Hispallae datio, deminutio, gentis enuptio, tutoris optio item esset quasi ei vir testamento dedisset; utique ei ingenuo nubere liceret, neu quid ei qui eam duxisset ob id fraudi ignominiaeve esset*' – that Fecenia Hispalla shall have the right to dispose of her property, to decrease it, to marry outside the gens, and to choose for herself a guardian exactly as if her (deceased) husband had conferred this right on her by testament; that she may marry a freeman, and that the man who takes her to wife shall not be considered to have committed a wrongful or shameful act thereby.

Without a doubt, Fecenia, a freedwoman, is here granted the right to marry outside the gens. And equally without a doubt the husband possessed the right, according to this passage, to bequeath to his wife by will the right to marry outside the gens after his death. But outside *which* gens?

If the woman had to marry within her gens, as Mommsen asssumes, she remained within this gens also after her marriage. But in the first place the endogamous character of the gens which is here asserted is precisely what has to be proved. And, secondly, if the wife had to marry within the gens, then, of course, so had the man, for otherwise he could not get a wife. So we reach the position that the man could bequeath to his wife by will a right which he himself and for himself did not possess; we arrive at a legal absurdity. Mommsen also feels this, and hence makes the assumption: 'For a lawful marriage outside the gens, it was probably necessary to have the consent, not only of the chief, but of all members of the gens.' That is a very bold assumption in the first place, and, secondly, it contradicts the clear wording of the passage. The senate grants her this right *in the place of her husband*; it grants her expressly neither more nor less than her husband could have granted her, but what it grants her is an *absolute* right, conditional upon no other restriction. Thus it is provided that if she makes use of this right, her new husband also shall not suffer any disability. The senate even directs the present and future consuls and praetors to see to it that no injurious consequences to her follow. Mommsen's assumption therefore seems to be completely inadmissible.

Or assume that the woman married a man from another

gens, but herself remained in the gens into which she had been born. Then, according to the above passage, the man would have had the right to allow his wife to marry outside her own gens. That is, he would have had the right to make dispositions in the affairs of a gens to which he did not even belong. The thing is so patently absurd that we need waste no more words on it.

Hence there only remains the assumption that in her first marriage the woman married a man from another gens and thereby immediately entered the gens of her husband, which Mommsen himself actually admits to have been the practice when the woman married outside her gens. Then everything at once becomes clear. Severed from her old gens by her marriage and accepted into the gentile group of her husband, the woman occupies a peculiar position in her new gens. She is, indeed, a member of the gens, but not related by blood. By the mere manner of her acceptance as a gentile member, she is entirely excluded from the prohibition against marrying within the gens, for she has just married into it. Further, she is accepted as one of the married members of the gens, and on her husband's death inherits from his property, the property of a gentile member. What is more natural than that this property should remain within the gens and that she should therefore be obliged to marry a member of her husband's gens and nobody else? And if an exception is to be made, who is so competent to give her the necessary authorization as the man who has bequeathed her this property, her first husband? At the moment when he bequeaths to her a part of his property and at the same time allows her to transfer it into another gens through marriage or in consequence of marriage, this property still belongs to him and he is therefore literally disposing of his own property. As regards the woman herself and her relation to her husband's gens, it was he who brought her into the gens by a free act of will – the marriage. Hence it also seems natural that he should be the proper person to authorize her to leave this gens by a second marriage. In a word, the matter appears simple and natural as soon as we abandon the extraordinary conception of the endogamous Roman gens and regard it, with Morgan, as originally exogamous.

There still remains one last assumption which has also found adherents, and probably the most numerous. On this view, the passage in Livy only means that 'freed servants (*libertae*) could not without special permission *e gente enubere* (marry out of the gens) or perform any of the acts, which involving the slightest loss of rights (*capitis deminutio minima*), would have resulted in the *liberta* leaving the gens' (Lange, *Römische Altertümer*, Berlin, 1856, 1, p. 195, where Huschke is cited in connection with our passage from Livy). If this supposition is correct, the passage then proves nothing at all about the position of free Roman women, and there can be even less question of any obligation resting on them to marry within the gens.

The expression *enuptio gentis* only occurs in this one passage and nowhere else in the whole of Latin literature. The word *enubere*, to marry outside, only occurs three times, also in Livy, and then not in reference to the gens. The fantastic notion that Roman women were only allowed to marry within their gens owes its existence solely to this one passage. But it cannot possibly be maintained. For either the passage refers to special restrictions for freedwomen, in which case it proves nothing about free women (*ingenuae*), or it applies also to free women; and then it proves, on the contrary, that the woman married as a rule outside her gens but on her marriage entered into the gens of her husband, which contradicts Mommsen and supports Morgan.

Almost three centuries after the foundation of Rome, the gentile groups were still so strong that a patrician gens, that of the Fabii, was able to undertake an independent campaign with the permission of the senate against the neighbouring town of Veii; 306 Fabii are said to have set out and to have been killed to a man in an ambush; according to the story, only one boy who had remained behind survived to propagate the gens.

As we have said, ten gentes formed a phratry, which among the Romans was called a *curia* and had more important public functions than the Greek phratry. Every *curia* had its own religious rites, shrines and priests; the latter as a body formed one of the Roman priestly colleges. Ten *curiae* formed a tribe, which probably like the rest of the Latin tribes originally had an elected president – military leader and high priest. The three tribes together formed the Roman people, the *populus Romanus*.

Thus no one could belong to the Roman people unless he was a member of a gens and through it of a *curia* and a tribe. The first constitution of the Roman people was as follows: public affairs were managed in the first instance by the senate, which, as Niebuhr first rightly saw, was composed of the presidents of the 300 gentes; it was because they were the elders of the gens that they were called fathers, *patres*, and their body, the senate (council of the elders, from *senex*, old). Here again the custom of electing always from the same family in the gens brought into being the first hereditary nobility. These families called themselves 'patricians' and claimed for themselves exclusive right of entry into the senate and tenure of all other offices. The acquiescence of the people in this claim in course of time and its transformation into an actual right, appear in legend as the story that Romulus conferred the patriciate and its privileges on the first senators and their descendants. The senate, like the Athenian *boulè*, made final decisions in many matters and held preparatory discussions on those of greater importance, particularly new laws. With regard to these, the decision rested with the assembly of the people called the *comitia curiata* (assembly of the *curiae*). The people assembled together grouped in *curiae*, each *curia* probably grouped in gentes; each of the 30 *curiae* had one vote in the final decision. The assembly of the *curiae* accepted or rejected all laws, elected all higher officials including the *rex* (so-called king), declared war (the senate, however, concluded peace), and as supreme court, decided on the appeal of the parties concerned all cases involving death sentence on a Roman citizen. Lastly, besides the senate and the assembly of the people, there was the *rex*, who corresponded exactly to the Greek *basileus* and was not at all the almost absolute king which Mommsen made him out to be.* He also was military leader, high priest, and president of certain courts. He had no civil authority whatever, nor any power over the life, liberty, or property of citizens, except such as derived from his disciplinary powers as military leader or his executive powers as president of a court. The office of *rex* was not hereditary; on the contrary, he was first elected by the assembly of the *curiae* probably on the nomination of his predecessor, and then at a second meeting solemnly installed in office. That he could also be deposed is shown by the fate of Tarquinius Superbus.

Like the Greeks of the heroic age, the Romans in the age of the so-called kings lived in a military democracy founded on gentes, phratries, and tribes and developed out of them. Even if the *curiae* and tribes were to a certain extent artificial groups, they were formed after the genuine, primitive models of the society out of which they had arisen and by which they were still surrounded on all sides. Even if the primitive patrician nobility had already gained ground, even if the *reges* were endeavouring gradually to extend their power, it does not change the original, fundamental character of the constitution, and that alone matters.

Meanwhile, Rome and the Roman territory, which had been enlarged by conquest, increased in population partly through immigration, partly through the addition of inhabitants of the subjugated, chiefly Latin, districts. All these new citizens of the state (we leave aside the question of the clients) stood outside the old gentes, *curiae*, and tribes, and therefore formed no part of the *populus Romanus*, the real Roman people.

* The Latin *rex* is the same as the Celtic-Irish *righ* (tribal chief) and the Gothic *reiks*. That *reiks* signified head of the gens or tribe, as did also originally the German word *Fürst* (meaning 'first' – *cf.* English *first* and Danish *förste*), is shown by the fact that already in the fourth century the Goths had a special word for the later 'king', the military leader of the whole people: *thiudans*. In Ulfilas' translation of the Bible, Artaxerxes and Herod are never called *reiks*, but *thiudans*, and the empire of Emperor Tiberius is not called *reiki*, but *thiudinassus*. In the name of the Gothic *thiudans* or, as we inaccurately translate, 'king', Thiudareik (Theodorich, *i.e.* Dietrich), both titles coalesce.

They were personally free, could own property in land, and had to pay taxes and do military service. But they could not hold any office, nor take part in the assembly of the *curiae*, nor share in the allotment of conquered state lands. They formed the class that was excluded from all public rights, the *plebs*. Owing to their continually increasing numbers, their military training and their possession of arms, they became a powerful threat to the old *populus*, which now rigidly barred any addition to its own ranks from outside. Further, landed property seems to have been fairly equally divided between *populus* and *plebs*, while the commercial and industrial wealth, though not as yet much developed, was probably for the most part in the hands of the *plebs*.

The great obscurity which envelops the completely legendary primitive history of Rome – an obscurity considerably deepened by the rationalistically pragmatical interpretations and accounts given of the subject by later authors with legalistic minds – makes it impossible to say anything definite about the time, course, or occasion of the revolution which made an end of the old gentile constitution. All that is certain is that its cause lay in the struggles between *plebs* and *populus*.

The new constitution, which was attributed to the *rex* Servius Tullius and followed the Greek model, particularly that of Solon, created a new assembly of the people in which *populus* and plebeians without distinction were included or excluded according to whether they performed military service or not. The whole male population liable to bear arms was divided on a property basis into six classes. The lower limit in each of the five classes was: (1) 100,000 asses, (2) 75,000 asses, (3) 50,000 asses, (4) 25,000 asses, (5) 11,000 asses, according to Dureau de la Malle, the equivalent to about 14,000, 10,500, 7,000, 3,600, and 1,570 marks respectively. The sixth class, the proletarians, consisted of those with less property than the lowest class and those exempt from military service and taxes. In the new popular assembly of the centuries (*comitia centuriata*), the citizens appeared in military formation arranged by companies in their centuries of 100 men, each century having one vote. Now the first class put 80 centuries in the field, the second 22, the third 20, the fourth 22, the fifth 30, and the sixth also one century for the sake of appearances. In addition, there was the cavalry, drawn from the wealthiest men, with 18 centuries – total, 193; 97 votes were thus required for a clear majority. But the cavalry and the first class alone had together 98 votes and therefore the majority; if they were agreed, they did not ask the others; they made their decision, and it stood.

This new assembly of the centuries now took over all political rights of the former assembly of the *curiae*, with the exception of a few nominal privileges. The *curiae* and the gentes of which they were composed were thus degraded as in Athens to mere private and religious associations and continued to vegetate as such for a long period, while the assembly of the *curiae* soon became completely dormant. In order that the three old tribes of kinship should also be excluded from the state, four local tribes were instituted, each of which inhabited one quarter of the city and possessed a number of political rights.

Thus in Rome also, even before the abolition of the so-called monarchy, the old order of society based on personal ties of blood was destroyed and in its place was set up a new and complete state constitution based on territorial division and difference of wealth. Here the public power consisted of the body of citizens liable to military service, in opposition not only to the slaves but also to those excluded from service in the army and from possession of arms, the so-called proletarians.

The banishment of the last *rex*, Tarquinius Superbus, who usurped real monarchic power, and the replacement of the office of *rex* by two military leaders (consuls) with equal powers (as among the Iroquois) was simply a further development of this new constitution. Within this new constitution, the whole history of the Roman republic runs its course with all the struggles between patricians and plebeians for admission to office and share in the state lands, and the final merging of the patrician nobility in the new class of the great land and money owners, who, gradually swallowing up all the land of the peasants ruined by military service, employed slave labour to cultivate the enormous estates thus formed, depopulated Italy and so threw open the door not only to the emperors but also to their successors, the German barbarians.

CHAPTER VII

The Gens among Celts and Germans

Space does not allow us to consider the gentile institutions still existing in greater or lesser degree of purity among the most various savage and barbarian peoples, nor the traces of these institutions in the ancient history of the civilized peoples of Asia. The institutions or their traces are found everywhere. A few examples will be enough. Before the gens had been recognized, the man who took the greatest pains to misunderstand it, McLennan himself, proved its existence and in the main accurately described it among the Kalmucks, Circassians, Samoyeds and three Indian peoples: the Warali, Magars and Munniporees. Recently it has been discovered and described by M. Kovalevsky among the Pshavs, Shevsurs, Svanets and other Caucasian tribes. Here we will only give some short notes on the occurrence of the gens among Celts and Germans.

The oldest Celtic laws which have been preserved show the gens still fully alive. In Ireland, after being forcibly broken up by the English, it still lives today in the consciousness of the people, as an instinct at any rate. In Scotland it was still in full strength in the middle of the eighteenth century, and here again it succumbed only to the weapons, laws, and courts of the English.

The old Welsh laws which were recorded in writing several centuries before the English conquest, at the latest in the eleventh century, still show common tillage of the soil by whole villages, even if only as an exceptional relic of a once general custom. Each family had five acres for its own cultivation; a piece of land was cultivated collectively as well

and the yield shared. In view of the analogy of Ireland and
Scotland, it cannot be doubted that these village communities
represent gentes or subdivisions of gentes, even though
further examination of the Welsh laws, which I cannot
undertake for lack of time (my notes date from 1869), should
not provide direct proof. But what is directly proved by the
Welsh sources and by the Irish is that among the Celts in the
eleventh century pairing marriage had not by any means
been displaced by monogamy.

In Wales a marriage only became indissoluble, or rather it
only ceased to be terminable by notification, after seven years
had elapsed. If the time was short of seven years by only
three nights, husband and wife could separate. They then
shared out their property between them; the woman divided
and the man chose. The furniture was divided according to
fixed and very humorous rules. If it was the man who
dissolved the marriage, he had to give the woman back her
dowry and some other things; if it was the woman, she
received less. Of the children the man took two and the
woman one, the middle child. If after the separation the
woman took another husband and the first husband came to
fetch her back again, she had to follow him even if she had
already *one* foot in her new marriage bed. If, on the other
hand, the man and woman had been together for seven years,
they were husband and wife, even without any previous
formal marriage. Chastity of girls before marriage was not at
all strictly observed, nor was it demanded; the provisions in
this respect are of an extremely frivolous character and not at
all in keeping with bourgeois morality. If a woman committed
adultery, the husband had the right to beat her (this was one
of the three occasions when he was allowed to do so;
otherwise he was punished), but not then to demand any
other satisfaction since 'for the one offence there shall be
either atonement or vengeance, but not both' [Ancient Laws
of Institutes of Wales, I, 1841, p. 93]. The grounds on which
the wife could demand divorce without losing any of her
claims in the subsequent settlement were very comprehen-
sive; if the husband had bad breath, it was enough. The

money which had to be paid to the chief of the tribe or king to buy off his right of the first night (*gobr merch*, whence the medieval name, *marcheta*; French *marquette*) plays a large part in the code of laws. The women had the right to vote in the assemblies of the people. When we add that the evidence shows similar conditions in Ireland; that there, also, temporary marriages were quite usual and that at the separation very favourable and exactly defined conditions were assured to the woman, including even compensation for her domestic services; that in Ireland there was a 'first wife' as well as other wives, and that in the division of an inheritance no distinction was made between children born in wedlock or outside it – we then have a picture of pairing marriage in comparison with which the form of marriage observed in North America appears strict. This is not surprising in the eleventh century among a people who even so late as Caesar's time were still living in group marriage.

The existence of the Irish gens (*sept*; the tribe was called *clainne*, clan) is confirmed and described not only by the old legal codes, but also by the English jurists of the seventeenth century who were sent over to transform the clan lands into domains of the English crown. Until then, the land had been the common property of the clan or gens in so far as the chieftains had not already converted it into their private domains. When a member of the gens died and a household consequently came to an end, the gentile chief (the English jurists called him *caput cognationis*) made a new division of the whole territory among the remaining households. This must have been done, broadly speaking, according to the rules in force in Germany. Forty or fifty years ago village fields were very numerous, and even today a few of these 'rundales', as they are called, may still be found. The peasants of a rundale, now individual tenants on the soil that had been the common property of the gens till it was seized by the English conquerors, pay rent for their respective piece of land but put all their shares in arable and meadowland together, which they then divide according to position and quality into *Gewanne*, as they are called on the Moselle, each receiving a share in each *Gewann*; moorland and pastureland are used in common. Only fifty years ago new divisions were still made from time to time, sometimes annually. The field-map of such a village looks exactly like that of a German *Gehöferschaft* [peasant community] on the Moselle or in the Hochwald. The gens also lives on in the 'fractions'. The Irish peasants often divide themselves into parties based apparently on perfectly absurd or meaningless distinctions; to the English they are quite incomprehensible and seem to have no other purpose than the favourite ceremony of two factions hammering one another. They are artificial revivals, modern substitutes for the dispersed gentes, manifesting in their own peculiar manner the persistence of the inherited gentile instinct. In some districts the members of the gens still live pretty much together on the old territory; in the thirties the great majority of the inhabitants of County Monaghan still had only four family names, that is, they were descended from four gentes or clans. *

In Scotland the decay of the gentile organization dates from the suppression of the rising of 1745. The precise function of the Scottish clan in this organization still awaits investigation; but that the clan is a gentile body is beyond doubt. In

* During a few days spent in Ireland [September 1891], I realized afresh to what an extent the country people still live in the conceptions of the gentile period. The landed proprietor, whose tenant the farmer is, is still regarded by the latter as a kind of chief of the clan whose duty it is to manage the land in the interests of all while the farmer pays tribute in the form of rent, but has a claim upon him for assistance in times of necessity. Similarly, everyone who is well-off is considered under an obligation to assist his poorer neighbours when they fall on hard times. Such help is not charity; it is what the poorer member of the clan is entitled to receive from the wealthier member or the chief. One can understand the complaints of the political economists and jurists about the impossibility of making the Irish peasant grasp the idea of modern bourgeois property; the Irishman simply cannot get it into his head that there can be property with rights but no duties. But one can also understand that when Irishmen with these naive gentile conceptions suddenly find themselves in one of the big English or American towns among a population with completely different ideas of morality and justice, they easily become completely confused about both morality and justice and lose all their bearings, with the result that masses of them become demoralized. [*Note to the Fourth Edition.*]

Walter Scott's novels the Highland clan lives before our eyes. It is, says Morgan:

... an excellent type of the gens in organization and in spirit, and an extraordinary illustration of the power of the gentile life over its members ... We find in their feuds and blood revenge, in their localization by gentes, in their use of lands in common, in the fidelity of the clansman to his chief and of the members of the clan to each other, the usual and persistent features of gentile society ... Descent was in the male line, the children of the males remaining members of the clan, while the children of its female members belonged to the clans of their respective fathers [pp. 368–9].

But that formerly mother right prevailed in Scotland is proved by the fact that, according to Bede, in the royal family of the Picts succession was in the female line. Among the Scots, as among the Welsh, a relic even of the punaluan family persisted into the Middle Ages in the form of the right of the first night which the head of the clan or the king, as last representative of the former community of husbands, had the right to exercise with every bride, unless it was compounded for money.

That the Germans were organized in gentes until the time of the migrations is beyond all doubt. They could have occupied the territory between the Danube, Rhine, Vistula, and the northern seas only a few centuries before our era; the Cimbri and Teutons were then still in full migration and the Suevi did not find any permanent habitation until Caesar's time. Caesar expressly states of them that they had settled in gentes and kindreds (*gentibus cognationibusque*), and in the mouth of a Roman of the Julian gens the word *gentibus* has a definite meaning which cannot be argued away. The same was true of all the Germans; they seem still to have settled by gentes even in the provinces they conquered from the Romans. The code of laws of the Alemanni confirms that the people settled by kindreds (*genealogiae*) in the conquered territory south of the Danube; *genealogia* is used in exactly the same sense as *Markgenossenschaft* or *Dorfgenossenschaft* [mark or village community] later. Kovalevsky has recently put forward the view that these *genealogiae* are the large household communities among which the land was divided and from which the village community only developed later. This would then probably also apply to the *fara*, with which expression the Burgundians and the Lombards – that is, a Gothic and a Herminonian or High German tribe – designated nearly, if not exactly, the same thing as the *genealogia* in the Alemannian code of laws. Whether it is really a gens or a household community must be settled by further research.

The records of language leave us in doubt whether all the Germans had a common expression for gens, and what that expression was. Etymologically, the Gothic *kuni*, Middle High German *künne*, corresponds to the Greek *genos* and the Latin *gens* and is used in the same sense. The fact that the term for woman comes from the same root – Greek *gyne*, Slav *zena*, Gothic *qvino*, Old Norse *kona, kuna* – points back to the time of mother right. Among the Lombards and Burgundians we find, as already mentioned, the term *fara* which Grimm derives from an imaginary root *fisan*, to beget. I should prefer to go back to the more obvious derivation from *faran* (*fahren*), to travel or wander; *fara* would then denote a section of the migrating people which remained permanently together and almost as a matter of course would be composed of relatives. In the several centuries of migration, first to the east and then to the west, the expression came to be transferred to the kinship group itself. There are, further, the Gothic *sibja*, Anglo-Saxon *sib*, Old High German *sippia, sippa, sippe* [kindred]. Old Norse only has the plural *sifjar*, relatives; the singular only occurs as the name of a goddess, *Sif*. Lastly, still another expression occurs in the *Hildebrandslied*, where Hildebrand asks Hadubrand: 'Who is thy father among the men of the people . . . or of what kin art thou?' (*eddo huêlîhes cnuosles du sîs*). In as far as there was a common German name for the gens, it was probably the Gothic *kuni* that was used; this is rendered probable, not only by its identity with the corresponding expression in the related languages, but also by the fact that from it is derived the word *kuning, König*

171

(king), which originally denotes the head of a gens or of a tribe. *Sibja*, *Sippe*, does not seem to call for consideration; at any rate *sifjar* in Old Norse denotes not only blood relations but also relations by marriage; thus it includes the members of at least *two* gentes, and hence *sif* itself cannot have been the term for the gens.

As among the Mexicans and Greeks, so also among the Germans the order of battle, both the cavalry squadrons and the wedge formations of the infantry, was drawn up by gentes. Tacitus' use of the vague expression 'by families and kindreds' is to be explained through the fact that in his time gens in Rome had long ceased to be a living body.

A further passage in Tacitus is decisive. It states that the maternal uncle looks upon his nephew as his own son, and that some even regard the bond of blood between the maternal uncle and the nephew as more sacred and close than that between father and son, so that when hostages are demanded the sister's son is considered a better security than the natural son of the man whom it is desired to bind. Here we have living evidence described as particularly characteristic of the Germans of the matriarchal, and therefore primitive, gens.*
If a member of such a gens gave his own son as a pledge of his oath and the son then paid the penalty of death for his father's breach of faith, the father had to answer for that to himself. But if it was a sister's son who was sacrificed, then the most sacred law of the gens was violated. The member of

* The peculiar closeness of the bond between maternal uncle and nephew, which derives from the time of mother right and is found among many peoples, is only recognized by the Greeks in their mythology of the heroic age. According to Diodorus (IV, 34), Meleager slays the sons of Thestius, the brothers of his mother Althaea. She regards this deed as such an inexpiable crime that she curses the murderer, her own son, and prays for his death. 'The gods heard her wishes,' the story says, 'and put an end to Meleager's life.' Also according to Diodorus (IV, 44), the Argonauts land in Thrace under Heracles and there find that Phineus, at the instigation of his new wife, is shamefully maltreating the two sons born to him by his former wife, the Boread Cleopatra, whom he has put away. But among the Argonauts there are also Boreads, brothers of Cleopatra, therefore maternal uncles of the maltreated boys. They at once take up their nephews' cause, free them, and kill their guards.

the gens who was nearest of kin to the boy or youth, and more than all others was bound to protect him, was guilty of his death; either he should not have pledged him or he should have kept the agreement. Even if we had no other trace of gentile organization among the Germans, this one passage would suffice.

Still more decisive, because it comes about 800 years later, is a passage from the Old Norse poem of the twilight of the gods and the end of the world, the *Völuspá*. In this 'vision of the seeress', into which Christian elements are also interwoven, as Bang and Bugge have now proved, the description of the period of universal degeneration and corruption leading up to the great catastrophe contains the following passage:

> *Broedhr munu berjask*   *ok at bönum verdask,*
> *munu systrungar*   *sifjum spilla.*

'Brothers will make war upon one another and become one another's murderers, *the children of sisters* will break kinship.' *Systrungar* means the son of the mother's sister, and that these sisters' sons should betray the blood bond between them is regarded by the poet as an even greater crime than that of fratricide. The force of the climax is in the word *systrungar*, which emphasizes the kinship on the mother's side; if the word had been *syskina-börn*, brothers' or sisters' children, or *syskinasynir*, brothers' or sisters' sons, the second line would not have been a climax to the first but would merely have weakened the effect. Hence even in the time of the Vikings when the *Völuspá* was composed, the memory of mother right had not yet been obliterated in Scandinavia.

In the time of Tacitus, however, mother right had already given way to father right, at least among the Germans with whose customs he was more familiar. The children inherited from the father; if there were no children, the brothers and the uncles on the father's and the mother's side. The fact that the mother's brother was allowed to inherit is connected with the survivals of mother right already mentioned and again proves how new father right still was among the Germans at that time. Traces of mother right are also found until late in the Middle Ages. Apparently even at that time people still did not have any great trust in fatherhood, especially in the case of serfs. When, therefore, a feudal lord demanded from a town the return of a fugitive serf, it was required – for example, in Augsburg, Basle and Kaiserlautern – that the accused person's status as serf should be sworn to by six of his nearest blood relations, and that they should all be relations on the mother's side (Maurer, *Städteverfassung*, I, p. 381).

Another relic of mother right, which was still only in process of dying out, was the respect of the Germans for the female sex which to the Romans was almost incomprehensible. Young girls of noble family were considered the most binding hostages in treaties with the Germans. The thought that their wives and daughters might be taken captive and carried into slavery was terrible to them and more than anything else fired their courage in battle; they saw in a woman something holy and prophetic and listened to her advice even in the most important matters. Veleda, the priestess of the Bructerians on the River Lippe, was the very soul of the whole Batavian rising in which Civilis, at the head of the Germans and Belgae, shook the foundations of Roman rule in Gaul. In the home, the woman seems to have held undisputed sway, though together with the old people and the children she also had to do all the work while the man hunted, drank, or idled about. That, at least, is what Tacitus says; but as he does not say who tilled the fields and definitely declares that the serfs only paid tribute but did not have to render labour dues, the bulk of the adult men must have had to do what little work the cultivation of the land required.

The form of marriage, as already said, was a pairing marriage which was gradually approaching monogamy. It was not yet strict monogamy, as polygamy was permitted for the leading members of the tribe. In general, strict chastity was required of the girls (in contrast to the Celts), and Tacitus also speaks with special warmth of the sacredness of the marriage tie among the Germans. Adultery by the woman is the only ground for divorce mentioned by him. But there are many gaps in his report, and it is also only too apparent that he is holding up a mirror of virtue before the dissipated Romans. One thing is certain: if the Germans were such paragons of virtue in their forests, it only required slight contact with the outside world to bring them down to the level of the average man in the rest of Europe. Amidst the Roman world, the last trace of moral austerity disappeared far more rapidly even than the German language. For proof it is enough to read Gregory of Tours. That in the German primeval forests there could be no such voluptuous abandonment to all the refinements of sensuality as in Rome is obvious; the superiority of the Germans to the Roman world in this respect also is sufficiently great, and there is no need to endow them with an ideal continence in things of the flesh, such as has never yet been practised by an entire nation.

Also derived from the gentile organization is the obligation to inherit the enmities as well as the friendships of the father or the relatives – likewise the *wergeld*, the fine for killing or injuring, in place of blood revenge. The *wergeld*, which only a generation ago was regarded as a specifically German institution, has now been shown to be general among hundreds of peoples as a milder form of the blood revenge originating out of the gentile organization. We find it, for example, among the American Indians, who also regard hospitality as an obligation. Tacitus' description of hospitality as practised among the Germans (*Germania*, Ch. XXI) is identical almost to the details with that given by Morgan of his Indians.

The endless, burning controversy as to whether the Germans of Tacitus' time had already definitely divided the land or not, and how the relevant passages are to be interpreted, now belongs to the past. No more words need be wasted in this dispute since it has been established that among all peoples the cultivated land was tilled collectively by the gens and later by communistic household communities such as were still found by Caesar among the Suevi, and that after this stage the land was allotted to individual families with periodical repartitions, which are shown to have survived as a local custom in Germany down to our day. If in the 150 years between Caesar and Tacitus the Germans had changed from the collective cultivation of the land expressly attributed by Caesar to the Suevi (they had no divided or private fields whatever, he says) to individual cultivation with annual repartition of the land, that is surely progress enough. The transition from that stage to complete private property in land during such a short period and without any outside interference is a sheer impossibility. What I read in Tacitus is simply what he says in his own dry words: they change (or divide afresh) the cultivated land every year, and there is enough common land left over. It is the stage of agriculture and property relations in regard to the land which exactly corresponds to the gentile constitution of the Germans at that time.

I leave the preceding paragraph unchanged as it stood in the former editions. Meanwhile the question has taken another turn. Since Kovalevsky has shown [see p. 89] that the patriarchal household community was a very common, if not universal, intermediate form between the matriarchal communistic family and the modern isolated family, it is no longer a question of whether property in land is communal or private, which was the point at issue between Maurer and Waitz, but a question of the *form* of the communal property. There is no doubt at all that the Suevi in Caesar's time not only owned the land in common but also cultivated it in common for the common benefit. Whether the economic unit was the gens or the household community or a communistic kinship group intermediate between the two, or whether all three groups occurred according to the conditions of the soil – these questions will be in dispute for a long time to come. Kovalevsky maintains, however, that the conditions described by Tacitus presuppose the existence, not of the mark or village community, but of the household community and that the village community only develops out of the latter much later as a result of the increase in population.

According to this view, the settlements of the Germans in

the territory of which they were already in possession at the time of the Romans, and also in the territory which they later took from the Romans, were not composed of villages but of large household communities which included several generations, cultivated an amount of land proportionate to the number of their members, and had common use with their neighbours of the surrounding waste land. The passage in Tacitus about changing the cultivated land would then have to be taken in an agronomic sense: the community cultivated a different piece of land every year and allowed the land cultivated the previous year to lie fallow or run completely to waste; the population being scanty, there was always enough waste land left over to make any disputes about land unnecessary. Only in the course of centuries when the number of members in the household communities had increased so much that a common economy was no longer possible under the existing conditions of production, did the communities dissolve. The arable lands and meadowlands which had hitherto been common were divided in the manner familiar to us, first temporarily and then permanently among the single households which were now coming into being, while forest, pasture land, and water remained common.

In the case of Russia, this development seems to be a proved historical fact. With regard to Germany and, secondarily, the other Germanic countries, it cannot be denied that in many ways this view provides a better explanation of the sources and an easier solution to difficulties than that held hitherto, which takes the village community back to the time of Tacitus. On the whole, the oldest documents, such as the *Codex Laureshamensis*, can be explained much better in terms of the household community than of the village community. On the other hand, this view raises new difficulties and new questions which have still to be solved. They can only be settled by new investigations; but I cannot deny that in the case also of Germany, Scandinavia and England there is very great probability in favour of the intermediate form of the household community.

While in Caesar's time the Germans had only just taken up

or were still looking for settled abodes, in Tacitus' time they already had a full century of settled life behind them; correspondingly, the progress in the production of the necessities of life is unmistakable. They live in log houses; their clothing is still very much that of primitive people of the forests: coarse woollen mantles, skins; for women and notable people underclothing of linen. Their food is milk, meat, wild fruits and, as Pliny adds, oatmeal porridge (still the Celtic national food in Ireland and Scotland). Their wealth consists in cattle and horses, but of inferior breed; the cows are small, poor in build and without horns; the horses are ponies, with very little speed. Money was used rarely and in small amounts; it was exclusively Roman. They did not work gold or silver, nor did they value it. Iron was rare, and at least among the tribes on the Rhine and the Danube seems to have been almost entirely imported, not mined. Runic writing (imitated from the Greek or Latin letters) was a purely secret form of writing used only for religious magic. Human sacrifices were still offered. In short, we here see a people which had just raised itself from the middle to the upper stage of barbarism. But whereas the tribes living immediately on the Roman frontiers were hindered in the development of an independent metal and textile industry by the facility with which Roman products could be imported, such industry undoubtedly did develop in the north-east, on the Baltic. The fragments of weapons found in the Schleswig marshes – long iron sword, coat of mail, silver helmet and so forth, together with Roman coins of the end of the second century – and the German metal objects distributed by the migration show quite a pronounced character of their own, even when they derive from an originally Roman model. Emigration into the civilized Roman world put an end to this native industry everywhere except in England. With what uniformity this industry arose and developed can be seen, for example, in the bronze brooches; those found in Burgundy, Rumania and on the Sea of Azov might have come out of the same workshop as those found in England and Sweden and are just as certainly of Germanic origin.

The constitution also corresponds to the upper stage of barbarism. According to Tacitus, there was generally a council of chiefs (*principes*) which decided minor matters, but prepared more important questions for decision by the assembly of the people. At the lower stage of barbarism, so far as we have knowledge of it, as among the Americans, this assembly of the people still comprises only the members of the gens, not yet of the tribe or of the confederacy of tribes. The chiefs (*principes*) are still sharply distinguished from the military leaders (*duces*) just as they are among the Iroquois. They already subsist partially on gifts of cattle, corn, etc. from the members of the tribe; as in America they are generally elected from the same family. The transition to father right favoured, as in Greece and Rome, the gradual transformation of election into hereditary succession and hence the rise of a noble family in each gens. This old so-called tribal nobility disappeared for the most part during the migrations or soon afterward. The military leaders were chosen without regard to their descent, solely according to their ability. They had little power and had to rely on the force of example. Tacitus expressly states that the actual disciplinary authority in the army lay with the priests. The real power was in the hands of the assembly of the people. The king or the chief of the tribe presides; the people decide: 'No' by murmurs, 'Yes' by acclamation and clash of weapons. The assembly of the people is at the same time an assembly of justice; here complaints are brought forward and decided and sentences of death passed, the only capital crimes being cowardice, treason against the people, and unnatural lust. Also in the gentes and other subdivisions of the tribe, all the members sit in judgement under the presidency of the chief, who as in all the early German courts can only have guided the proceedings and put questions; the actual verdict was always given among Germans everywhere by the whole community.

Confederacies of tribes had grown up since the time of Caesar. Some of them already had kings; the supreme military commander was already aiming at the position of tyrant, as among the Greeks and Romans, and sometimes secured it.

But these fortunate usurpers were not by any means absolute rulers; they were, however, already beginning to break the fetters of the gentile constitution. Whereas freed slaves usually occupied a subordinate position since they could not belong to any gens, as favourites of the new kings they often won rank, riches and honours. The same thing happened after the conquest of the Roman Empire by these military leaders, who now became kings of great countries. Among the Franks, slaves and freedmen of the king played a leading part first at the court and then in the state; the new nobility was to a great extent descended from them.

One institution particularly favoured the rise of kingship – the retinues. We have already seen among the American Indians how, side by side with the gentile constitution, private associations were formed to carry on wars independently. Among the Germans these private associations had already become permanent. A military leader who had made himself a name gathered around him a band of young men eager for booty whom he pledged to personal loyalty, giving the same pledge to them. The leader provided their keep, gave them gifts, and organized them on a hierarchic basis: a bodyguard and a standing troop for smaller expeditions, and a regular corps of officers for operations on a larger scale. Weak as these retinues must have been and as we in fact find them to be later – for example, under Odoacer in Italy – they were nevertheless the beginnings of the decay of the old freedom of the people and showed themselves to be such during and after the migrations. For in the first place they favoured the rise of monarchic power. In the second place, as Tacitus already notes, they could only be kept together by continual wars and plundering expeditions. Plunder became an end in itself. If the leader of the retinue found nothing to do in the neighbourhood, he set out with his men to other peoples where there was war and the prospect of booty. The German mercenaries who fought in great numbers under the Roman standard even against Germans were partly mobilized through these retinues. They already represent the first form of the system of *Landsknechte* [mercenary soldiers], the shame and curse of the Germans. When the Roman Empire had been conquered, these retinues of the kings formed the second main stock, after the unfree and the Roman courtiers, from which the later nobility was drawn.

In general then, the constitution of those German tribes which had combined into peoples was the same as had developed among the Greeks of the heroic age and the Romans of the so-called time of the kings: assembly of the people, council of the chiefs of the gentes, and military leader who is already striving for real monarchic power. It was the highest form of constitution which the gentile order could achieve; it was the model constitution of the upper stage of barbarism. If society passed beyond the limits within which this constitution was adequate, that meant the end of the gentile order; it was broken up and the state took its place.

CHAPTER VIII

The Formation of the State among the Germans

According to Tacitus, the Germans were a very numerous people. Caesar gives us an approximate idea of the strength of the separate German peoples; he places the number of the Usipetans and the Tencterans who appeared on the left bank of the Rhine at 180,000, women and children included. That is about 100,000 to one people,* already considerably more than, for instance, the total number of the Iroquois in their prime, when, no more than 20,000 strong, they were the terror of the whole country from the Great Lakes to the Ohio and the Potomac. On the map, if we try to group the better known peoples settled near the Rhine according to the evidence of the reports, a single people occupies the space of a Prussian government district – that is, about 10,000 square kilometres or 182 geographical square miles [about 4,000 square miles]. Now the Germania Magna [Greater Germany] of the Romans, which reached as far as the Vistula, had an area of 500,000 square kilometres in round figures. Reckoning the average number of each people at 100,000, the total population of Germania Magna would work out at 5,000,000; a considerable figure for a barbarian group of peoples, but compared with our conditions – ten persons to the square kilometre or about 550 to the geographical square mile –

* The number assumed here is confirmed by a statement of Diodorus about the Celts of Gaul: 'In Gaul dwell many peoples of varying strength. Among those that are greatest the number is about 200,000, among the smallest, 50,000' (Diodorus Siculus, V, 25) – on an average, therefore, 125,000. It can undoubtedly be assumed that owing to their higher stage of development the single peoples among the Gauls were rather larger than among the Germans.

extremely low. But that by no means exhausts the number of the Germans then living. We know that all along the Carpathians and down to the south of the Danube there were German peoples descended from Gothic tribes, such as the Bastarnians, Peucinians and others who were so numerous that Pliny classes them together as the fifth main tribe of the Germans. As early as 180 BC they make their appearance as mercenaries in the service of the Macedonian King Perseus, and in the first years of Augustus, still advancing, they almost reached Adrianople. If we estimate these at only 1,000,000, the probable total number of the Germans at the beginning of our era must have been at least 6,000,000.

After permanent settlements had been founded in Germany, the population must have grown with increasing rapidity; the advances in industry we mentioned are in themselves proof of this. The objects found in the Schleswig marshes date from the third century, according to the Roman coins discovered with them. At this time, therefore, there was already a developed metal and textile industry on the Baltic, brisk traffic with the Roman Empire and a certain degree of luxury among the more wealthy – all signs of denser population. But also at this time begins the general attack by the Germans along the whole line of the Rhine, the Roman wall and the Danube, from the North Sea to the Black Sea – direct proof of the continual growth and outward thrust of the population. For three centuries the fight went on, during which the whole main body of the Gothic peoples (with the exception of the Scandinavian Goths and the Burgundians) thrust south-east, forming the left wing on the long front of attack; in the centre the High Germans (Herminones) pushed forward down the upper Danube; and on the right wing the Ischaevonians, now called Franks, advanced along the Rhine; the Ingaevonians carried out the conquest of Britain. By the end of the fifth century an exhausted and bleeding Roman Empire lay helpless before the invading Germans.

In earlier chapters we were standing at the cradle of ancient Greek and Roman civilization. Now we stand at its grave. Rome had driven the levelling plane of its world rule over all the countries of the Mediterranean basin, and that for centuries. Except when Greek offered resistance, all natural languages had been forced to yield to a debased Latin. There were no more national differences, no more Gauls, Iberians, Ligurians, Noricans; all had become Romans. Roman administration and Roman law had everywhere broken up the old kinship groups and with them the last vestige of local and national independence. The half-baked culture of Rome provided no substitute; it expressed no nationality, only the lack of nationality. The elements of new nations were present everywhere; the Latin dialects of the various provinces were becoming increasingly differentiated; the natural boundaries which once had made Italy, Gaul, Spain, Africa independent territories were still there and still made themselves felt. But the strength was not there to fuse these elements into new nations; there was no longer a sign anywhere of capacity for development or power of resistance, to say nothing of creative energy. The enormous mass of humanity in the whole enormous territory was held together by one bond only – the Roman state; and the Roman state had become in the course of time their worst enemy and oppressor. The provinces had annihilated Rome; Rome itself had become a provincial town like the rest – privileged, but no longer the ruler, no longer the hub of the world empire, not even the seat of the emperors or sub-emperors who now lived in Constantinople, Treves, Milan. The Roman state had become a huge, complicated machine, exclusively for bleeding its subjects. Taxes, state imposts and tributes of every kind pressed the mass of the people always deeper into poverty; the pressure was intensified until the exactions of governors, tax collectors and armies made it unbearable. That was what the Roman state had achieved with its world rule. It gave as the justification of its existence that it maintained order within the empire and protected it against the barbarians without. But its order was worse than the worst disorder, and the citizens whom it claimed to protect against the barbarians longed for the barbarians to deliver them.

Social conditions were no less desperate. Already in the

last years of the republic the policy of Roman rule had been ruthlessly to exploit the provinces; the empire, far from abolishing this exploitation, had organized it. The more the empire declined, the higher rose the taxes and levies, the more shamelessly the officials robbed and extorted. The Romans had always been too occupied in ruling other nations to become proficient in trade and industry: it was only as usurers that they beat all who came before or after. What commerce had already existed and still survived was now ruined by official extortion; it struggled on only in the eastern, Greek part of the empire, which lies outside the present study. General impoverishment; decline of commerce, handicrafts and art; fall in the population; decay of the towns; relapse of agriculture to a lower level – such was the final result of Roman world rule.

Agriculture, always the decisive branch of production throughout the ancient world, was now more so than ever. In Italy the enormous estates (*latifundia*) which, since the end of the republic, occupied almost the whole country had been exploited in two different ways. They had been used either as pastures, the population being displaced by sheep and cattle which could be tended by a few slaves, or as country estates (*villae*) where large-scale horticulture was carried on with masses of slaves, partly as a luxury for the owner, partly for sale in the town markets. The great grazing farms had kept going and had probably even extended; the country estates and their gardens had been ruined through the impoverishment of their owners and the decay of the towns. The system of *latifundia* run by slave labour no longer paid; but at that time no other form of large-scale agriculture was possible. Small-scale production had again become the only profitable form. One country estate after another was cut up into small lots, which were handed over either to tenants who paid a fixed sum and had hereditary rights or to *partiarii*, stewards rather than tenants, who received a sixth or even only a ninth of the year's product in return for their labour. For the most part, however, these small lots of land were given out to *coloni* who paid for them a definite yearly

185

amount, were tied to the soil and could be sold together with their plot. True, they were not slaves, but neither were they free; they could not marry free persons, and their marriages with one another were not regarded as full marriages, but, like those of slaves, as mere concubinage (*contubernium*). They were the forerunners of the medieval serfs.

The slavery of classical times had outlived itself. Whether employed on the land in large-scale agriculture or in manufacture in the towns, it no longer yielded any satisfactory return – the market for its products was no longer there. But the small-scale agriculture and the small handicraft production to which the enormous production of the empire in its prosperous days was now shrunk had no room for numerous slaves. Only for the domestic and luxury slaves of the wealthy was there still a place in society. But though it was dying out, slavery was still common enough to make all productive labour appear to be work for slaves, unworthy of free Romans – and everybody was a free Roman now. Hence, on the one side, increasing manumissions of the superfluous slaves who were now a burden; on the other hand, a growth in some parts in the numbers of the *coloni* and in other parts of the declassed freemen (like the 'poor whites' in the ex-slave states of America). Christianity is completely innocent of the gradual dying out of ancient slavery; it was itself actively involved in the system for centuries under the Roman Empire and never interfered later with slave-trading by Christians – not with the Germans in the north or with the Venetians in the Mediterranean or with the later trade in Negroes.* Slavery no longer paid; it was for that reason it died out. But in dying it left behind its poisoned sting – the stigma attaching to the productive labour of freedmen. This was the blind alley from which the Roman world had no way out: slavery was economically impossible, the labour of freedmen was morally ostracized. The one could be the basic form of social produc-

---

* According to Bishop Liutprand of Cremona, in the tenth century the chief industry of Verdun – in the Holy German Empire, observe – was the manufacture of eunuchs who were exported at great profit to Spain for the Moorish harems.

tion no longer; the other, not yet. Nothing could help here except a complete revolution.

Things were no better in the provinces. We have most material about Gaul. Here there was still a free small peasantry in addition to *coloni*. In order to be secured against oppression by officials, judges, and usurers, these peasants often placed themselves under the protection, the patronage, of a powerful person; and it was not only individuals who did so, but whole communities, so that in the fourth century the emperors frequently prohibited the practice. But what help was this protection to those who sought it? Their patron made it a condition that they should transfer to him the rights of ownership in their pieces of land in return for which he guaranteed them the use of the land for their lifetime – a trick which the Holy Church took note of and in the ninth and tenth centuries lustily imitated, to the increase of God's glory and its own lands. At this time, it is true, about the year 475, Bishop Salvianus of Marseilles still inveighs indignantly against such theft. He relates that oppression by Roman officials and great landlords had become so heavy that many 'Romans' fled into districts already occupied by the barbarians and that the Roman citizens settled there feared nothing so much as a return to Roman rule. That parents owing to their poverty often sold their children into slavery at this time is proved by a decree prohibiting the practice.

In return for liberating the Romans from their own state, the German barbarians took from them two thirds of all the land and divided it among themselves. The division was made according to the gentile constitution. The conquerors being relatively few in number, large tracts of land were left undivided, as the property partly of the whole people, partly of the individual tribes and gentes. Within each gens the arable land and meadowland was distributed by lot in equal portions among the individual households. We do not know whether reallotments of the land were repeatedly carried out at this time, but in any event they were soon discontinued in the Roman provinces and the individual lots became alienable private property, *allodium*. Woods and pastures remained undivided for common use; the provisions regulating their common use and the manner in which the divided land was to be cultivated were settled in accordance with ancient custom and by the decision of the whole community. The longer the gens remained settled in its village and the more the Germans and the Romans gradually merged, the more the bond of union lost its character of kinship and became territorial. The gens was lost in the mark community, in which, however, traces of its origin in the kinship of its members are often enough still visible. Thus, at least in those countries where the mark community maintained itself – northern France, England, Germany and Scandinavia – the gentile constitution changed imperceptibly into a local constitution and thus became capable of incorporation into the state. But it nevertheless retained that primitive democratic character which distinguishes the whole gentile constitution, and thus even in its later enforced degeneration and up to the most recent times keeping something of the gentile constitution alive to be a weapon in the hands of the oppressed.

This weakening of the bond of blood in the gens followed from the degeneration of the organs of kinship also in the tribe and in the entire people as a result of their conquests. As we know, rule over subjugated peoples is incompatible with the gentile constitution. Here we can see this on a large scale. The German peoples, now masters of the Roman provinces, had to organize what they had conquered. But they could neither absorb the mass of Romans into the gentile bodies nor govern them through these bodies. At the head of the local Roman governing bodies, many of which continued for the time being to function, had to be placed a substitute for the Roman state, and this substitute could only be another state. The organs of the gentile constitution had to be transformed into state organs, and that very rapidly, for the situation was urgent. But the immediate representative of the conquering people was their military leader. To secure the conquered territory against attack from within and without, it was necessary to strengthen his power. The moment had come to transform the military leadership into kingship: the transformation was made.

Let us take the country of the Franks. Here the victorious Salian people had come into complete possession, not only of the extensive Roman state domains, but also of the very large tracts of land which had not been distributed among the larger and smaller district and mark communities, in particular all the larger forest areas. On his transformation from a plain military chief into the real sovereign of a country, the first thing which the king of the Franks did was to transform this property of the people into crown lands, to steal it from the people and to give it, outright or in fief, to his retainers. This retinue, which originally consisted of his personal following of warriors and of the other lesser military leaders, was presently increased not only by Romans – Romanized Gauls, whose education, knowledge of writing, familiarity with the spoken Romance language of the country and the written Latin language, as well as with the country's laws, soon made them indispensable to him – but also by slaves, serfs and freedmen, who composed his court and from whom he chose his favourites. All these received their portions of the people's land, at first generally in the form of gifts, later of benefices, usually conferred, to begin with, for the king's lifetime. Thus, at the expense of the people the foundation of a new nobility was laid.

And that was not all. The wide extent of the kingdom could not be governed with the means provided by the old gentile constitution; the council of chiefs, even if it had not long since become obsolete, would have been unable to meet, and it was soon displaced by the permanent retinue of the king. The old assembly of the people continued to exist in name, but it also increasingly became a mere assembly of military leaders subordinate to the king and of the new rising nobility. By the incessant civil wars and wars of conquest (the latter were particularly frequent under Charlemagne), the free land-owning peasants, the mass of the Frankish people, were reduced to the same state of exhaustion and penury as the Roman peasants in the last years of the republic. Though they had originally constituted the whole army and still remained its backbone after the conquest of France, by the beginning of the ninth century they were so impoverished that hardly one man in five could go to the wars. The army of free peasants raised directly by the king was replaced by an army composed of the servitors of the new nobles, including bondsmen, descendants of men who in earlier times had known no master save the king and still earlier no master at all, not even a king. The internal wars under Charlemagne's successors, the weakness of the authority of the crown, and the corresponding excesses of the nobles (including the *gau* counts [county administrators] instituted by Charlemagne, who were now striving to make their office hereditary) had already brought ruin on the Frankish peasantry, and the ruin was finally completed by the invasions of the Norsemen. Fifty years after the death of Charlemagne, the Empire of the Franks lay as defenceless at the feet of the Norsemen as the Roman Empire, 400 years earlier, had lain at the feet of the Franks.

Not only was there the same impotence against enemies from without, but there was almost the same social order or rather disorder within. The free Frankish peasants were in a plight similar to their predecessors, the Roman *coloni*. Plundered and ruined by wars, they had been forced to put themselves under the protection of the new nobles or of the Church, the crown being too weak to protect them. But they had to pay dearly for it. Like the Gallic peasants earlier, they had to transfer their rights of property in land to their protecting lord and received the land back from him in tenancies of various and changing forms, but always only in return for services and dues. Once in this position of dependence, they gradually lost their personal freedom also; after a few generations most of them were already serfs. How rapid was the disappearance of the free peasantry is shown by Irminon's records of the monastic possessions of the Abbey of Saint-Germain-des-Prés, at that time near, now in, Paris. On the huge holdings of this Abbey, which were scattered in the surrounding country, there lived in Charlemagne's time

2,788 households whose members were almost without exception Franks with German names. They included 2,080 *coloni*, 35 *liti* [semi-free peasants], 220 slaves, and only eight freehold tenants! The godless practice, as Salvianus had called it, by which the protecting lord had the peasant's land transferred to himself as his own property and only gave it back to the peasant for use during life, was now commonly employed by the Church against the peasants. The forced services now imposed with increasing frequency had had their prototype as much in the Roman *angariae*, compulsory labour for the state, as in the services provided by members of the German mark for bridge and road making and other common purposes. To all appearances, therefore, after 400 years the mass of the people were back again where they had started.

But that only proved two things: first, that the social stratification and the distribution of property in the declining Roman Empire completely correspond to the level of agricultural and industrial production at that time and had therefore been inevitable; secondly, that this level of production had neither risen nor fallen significantly during the following four centuries and had therefore with equal necessity again produced the same distribution of property and the same classes in the population. In the last centuries of the Roman Empire, the town had lost its former supremacy over the country, and in the first centuries of German rule it had not regained it. This implies a low level of development both in agriculture and industry. This general situation necessarily produces big ruling landowners and a dependent small peasantry. How impossible it was to graft on to such a society either the Roman system of *latifundia* worked by slave labour or the newer large-scale agriculture worked by forced services is proved by Charlemagne's experiments with the famous imperial country estates (*villae*). These experiments were gigantic in scope, but they left scarcely a trace. They were continued only by the monasteries, and only for them were they fruitful. But the monasteries were abnormal social bodies, founded on celibacy; they could produce exceptional results, but for that very reason necessarily continued to be exceptional themselves.

And yet progress was made during these 400 years. Though at the end we find almost the same main classes as at the beginning, the human beings who formed these classes were different. Ancient slavery had gone, and so had the pauper freedmen who despised work as only fit for slaves. Between the Roman *colonus* and the new bondsman had stood the free Frankish peasant. The 'useless memories and aimless strife' of decadent Roman culture were dead and buried. The social classes of the ninth century had been formed, not in the rottenness of a decaying civilization, but in the birth pangs of a new civilization. Compared with their Roman predecessors, the new breed, whether masters or servants, was a breed of men. The relation of powerful landowners and subject peasants which had meant for the ancient world the final ruin from which there was no escape was for them the starting point of a new development. And further, however unproductive these four centuries appear, *one* great product they did leave – the modern nationalities, the new forms and structures through which Western European humanity was to make coming history. The Germans had, in fact, given Europe new life, and therefore the break-up of the states in the Germanic period ended, not in subjugation by the Norsemen and Saracens, but in the further development of the system of benefices and protection into feudalism, and in such an enormous increase of the population that scarcely two centuries later the severe bloodletting of the Crusades was borne without injury.

But what was the mysterious magic by which the Germans breathed new life into a dying Europe? Was it some miraculous power innate in the Germanic race, such as our chauvinist historians romance about? Not a bit of it. The Germans, especially at that time, were a highly gifted Aryan tribe and in the full vigour of development. It was not, however, their specific national qualities which rejuvenated Europe, but simply – their barbarism, their gentile constitution.

Their individual ability and courage, their sense of freedom, their democratic instinct which in everything of public concern felt itself concerned; in a word all the qualities which had been lost to the Romans and were alone capable of forming new states and making new nationalities grow out of the slime of the Roman world – what else were they than the characteristics of the barbarian of the upper stage, fruits of his gentile constitution?

If they recast the ancient form of monogamy, moderated the supremacy of the man in the family, and gave the woman a higher position than the classical world had ever known, what made them capable of doing so if not their barbarism, their gentile customs, their living heritage from the time of mother right?

If in at least three of the most important countries, Germany, northern France and England, they carried over into the feudal state a genuine piece of gentile constitution in the form of mark communities, thus giving the oppressed class, the peasants, even under the harshest medieval serfdom a local centre of solidarity and a means of resistance such as neither the slaves of classical times nor the modern proletariat found ready to their hand – to what was this due, if not to their barbarism, their purely barbarian method of settlement in kinship groups?

Lastly, they were able to develop and make universal the milder form of servitude they had practised in their own country, which even in the Roman Empire increasingly displaced slavery; a form of servitude which, as Fourier first stressed, gives to the bondsmen the means of their gradual liberation as a *class* (*'fournit aux cultivateurs des moyens d'affranchissement collectif et progressif'*); a form of servitude which thus stands high above slavery, where the only possibility is the immediate release without any transitional stage of individual slaves (abolition of slavery by successful rebellion is unknown to antiquity), whereas the medieval serfs gradually won their liberation as a class. And to what do we owe this if not to their barbarism, thanks to which they had not yet reached the stage of fully developed slavery, neither the labour slavery of the classical world nor the domestic slavery of the Orient?

All the vigorous and creative life which the Germans infused into the Roman world was barbarism. Only barbarians are able to rejuvenate a world in the throes of collapsing civilization. And precisely the highest stage of barbarism, to which and in which the Germans worked their way upward before the migrations, was the most favourable for this process. That explains everything.

CHAPTER IX

Barbarism and Civilization

We have now traced the dissolution of the gentile constitution in the three great instances of the Greeks, the Romans, and the Germans. In conclusion, let us examine the general economic conditions which already undermined the gentile organization of society at the upper stage of barbarism and with the coming of civilization overthrew it completely. Here we shall need Marx's *Capital* as much as Morgan's book.

Arising in the middle stage of savagery, further developed during its upper stage, the gens reaches its most flourishing period, so far as our sources enable us to judge, during the lower stage of barbarism. We begin therefore with this stage.

Here – the American Indians must serve as our example – we find the gentile constitution fully formed. The tribe is now grouped in several gentes, generally two. With the increase in population, each of these original gentes splits up into several daughter gentes, their mother gens now appearing as the phratry. The tribe itself breaks up into several tribes, in each of which we find again, for the most part, the old gentes. The related tribes, at least in some cases, are united in a confederacy. This simple organization suffices completely for the social conditions out of which it sprang. It is nothing more than the grouping natural to those conditions, and it is capable of settling all conflicts that can arise within a society so organized. War settles external conflicts; it may end with the annihilation of the tribe but never with its subjugation. It is the greatness but also the limitation of the gentile constitution that it has no place for ruler and ruled. Within the tribe there is as yet no difference between rights and duties; the question whether participation in public affairs, in blood revenge or atonement, is a right or a duty does not exist for the Indian; it would seem to him just as absurd as the question whether it was a right or a duty to sleep, eat, or hunt. A division of the tribe or of the gens into different classes was equally impossible. And that brings us to the examination of the economic basis of these conditions.

The population is extremely sparse; it is dense only at the tribe's place of settlement, around which lie in a wide circle first the hunting grounds and then the protective belt of neutral forest which separates the tribe from others. The division of labour is purely primitive, between the sexes only. The man fights in the wars, goes hunting and fishing, procures the raw materials of food and the tools necessary for doing so. The woman looks after the house and the preparation of food and clothing, cooks, weaves, sews. They are each master in their own sphere: the man in the forest, the woman in the house. Each is owner of the instruments which he or she makes and uses: the man of the weapons, the hunting and fishing implements; the woman of the household gear. The housekeeping is communal among several and often many families.* What is made and used in common is common property – the house, the garden, the long boat. Here therefore, and here alone, there still exists in actual fact that 'property created by the owner's labour' which in civilized society is an ideal fiction of the jurists and economists, the last lying legal pretence by which modern capitalist property still bolsters itself up.

But humanity did not everywhere remain at this stage. In Asia they found animals which could be tamed and, when once tamed, bred. The wild buffalo cow had to be hunted; the tame buffalo cow gave a calf yearly and milk as well. A number of the most advanced tribes – the Aryans, Semites,

---

* Especially on the north-west coast of America – *see* Bancroft. Among the Haidahs on Queen Charlotte Islands there are households with as many as 700 persons under one roof. Among the Nootkas whole tribes used to live under one roof.

perhaps already also the Turanians – now made their chief work first the taming of cattle, later their breeding and tending only. Pastoral tribes separated themselves from the mass of the rest of the barbarians – *the first great social division of labour*. The pastoral tribes produced not only more necessities of life than the other barbarians, but different ones. They possessed the advantage over them of having not only milk, milk products and great supplies of meat, but also skins, wool, goat hair, and spun and woven fabrics, which became more common as the amount of raw material increased. Thus for the first time regular exchange became possible. At the earlier stages only occasional exchanges can take place; particular skill in the making of weapons and tools may lead to a temporary division of labour. Thus in many places undoubted remains of workshops for the making of stone tools have been found dating from the later Stone Age. The artists who here perfected their skill probably worked for the whole community, as each special handicraftsman still does in the gentile communities in India. In no case could exchange arise at this stage except within the tribe itself, and then only as an exceptional event. But now, with the differentiation of pastoral tribes, we find all the conditions ripe for exchange between branches of different tribes and its development into a regular established institution. Originally tribe exchanged with tribe through the respective chiefs of the gentes; but as the herds began to pass into private ownership, exchange between individuals became more common and, finally, the only form. Now the chief article which the pastoral tribes exchanged with their neighbours was cattle; cattle became the commodity by which all other commodities were valued and which was everywhere willingly taken in exchange for them – in short, cattle acquired a money function and already at this stage did the work of money. With such necessity and speed, even at the very beginning of commodity exchange, did the need for a money commodity develop.

Horticulture, probably unknown to Asiatic barbarians of the lower stage, was being practised by them in the middle stage at the latest, as the forerunner of agriculture. In the climate of the Turanian plateau, pastoral life is impossible without supplies of fodder for the long and severe winter. Here, therefore, it was essential that land should be put under grass and corn cultivated. The same is true of the steppes north of the Black Sea. But when once corn had been grown for the cattle, it also soon became food for men. The cultivated land still remained tribal property; at first it was allotted to the gens, later by the gens to the household communities and finally to individuals for use. The users may have had certain rights of possession, but nothing more.

Of the industrial achievements of this stage, two are particularly important. The first is the loom, the second the smelting of metal ores and the working of metals. Copper and tin, and their alloy, bronze, were by far the most important. Bronze provided serviceable tools and weapons though it could not displace stone tools; only iron could do that, and the method of obtaining iron was not yet understood. Gold and silver were beginning to be used for ornament and decoration and must already have acquired a high value as compared with copper and bronze.

The increase of production in all branches – cattle raising, agriculture, domestic handicrafts – gave human labour power the capacity to produce a larger product than was necessary for its maintenance. At the same time it increased the daily amount of work to be done by each member of the gens, household community or single family. It was now desirable to bring in new labour forces. War provided them; prisoners of war were turned into slaves. With its increase of the productivity of labour and therefore of wealth, and its extension of the field of production, the first great social division of labour was bound, in the general historical conditions prevailing, to bring slavery in its train. From the first great social division of labour arose the first great cleavage of society into two classes: masters and slaves, exploiters and exploited.

As to how and when the herds passed out of the common possession of the tribe or the gens into the ownership of individual heads of families, we know nothing at present.

But in the main it must have occurred during this stage. With the herds and the other new riches, a revolution came over the family. To procure the necessities of life had always been the business of the man; he produced and owned the means of doing so. The herds were the new means of producing these necessities; the taming of the animals in the first instance and their later tending were the man's work. To him, therefore, belonged the cattle and to him the commodities and the slaves received in exchange for cattle. All the surplus which the acquisition of the necessities of life now yielded fell to the man; the woman shared in its enjoyment, but had no part in its ownership. The 'savage' warrior and hunter had been content to take second place in the house, after the woman; the 'gentler' shepherd, in the arrogance of his wealth, pushed himself forward into the first place and the woman down into the second. And she could not complain. The division of labour within the family had regulated the division of property between the man and the woman. That division of labour had remained the same; and yet it now turned the previous domestic relation upside down simply because the division of labour outside the family had changed. The same cause which had ensured to the woman her previous supremacy in the house – that her activity was confined to domestic labour – this same cause now ensured the man's supremacy in the house. The domestic labour of the woman no longer counted beside the acquisition of the necessities of life by the man; the latter was everything, the former an unimportant extra. We can already see from this that to emancipate woman and make her the equal of the man is and remains an impossibility so long as the woman is shut out from social productive labour and restricted to private domestic labour. The emancipation of woman will only be possible when woman can take part in production on a large, social scale, and domestic work no longer claims anything but an insignificant amount of her time. And only now has that become possible through modern large-scale industry, which does not merely permit the employment of female labour over a wide range, but positively demands it, while it also tends toward ending private domestic labour by changing it more and more into a public industry.

The man now being actually supreme in the house, the last barrier to his absolute supremacy had fallen. This autocracy was confirmed and perpetuated by the overthrow of mother right, the introduction of father right, and the gradual transition of the pairing marriage into monogamy. But this tore a breach in the old gentile order; the single family became a power, and its rise was a menace to the gens.

The next step leads us to the upper stage of barbarism, the period when all civilized peoples have their heroic age: the age of the iron sword, but also of the iron ploughshare and axe. Iron was now at the service of man, the last and most important of all the raw materials which played a historically revolutionary role – until the potato. Iron brought about the tillage of large areas, the clearing of wide tracts of virgin forest; iron gave to the handicraftsman tools so hard and sharp that no stone, no other known metal, could resist them. All this came gradually; the first iron was often even softer than bronze. Hence stone weapons only disappeared slowly; not merely in the *Hildebrandslied*, but even as late as the battle of Hastings in 1066, stone axes were still used for fighting. But progress could not now be stopped; it went forward with fewer checks and greater speed. The town, with its houses of stone or brick encircled by stone walls, towers and ramparts, became the central seat of the tribe or the confederacy of tribes – an enormous architectural advance, but also a sign of growing danger and need for protection. Wealth increased rapidly, but as the wealth of individuals. The products of weaving, metalwork and the other handicrafts, which were becoming more and more differentiated, displayed growing variety and skill. In addition to corn, leguminous plants and fruits, agriculture now provided wine and oil, the preparation of which had been learned. Such manifold activities were no longer within the scope of one and the same individual; the *second great division of labour* took place – handicraft separated from agriculture. The continuous increase of production and simultaneously of the productivity of labour heightened the value of human labour power. Slavery, which during the preceding period was still in its beginnings and sporadic, now becomes an essential constituent part of the social system; slaves no longer merely help with production – they are driven by dozens to work in the fields and the workshops. With the splitting up of production into the two great main branches, agriculture and handicrafts, arises production directly for exchange, commodity production; with it came commerce, not only in the interior and on the tribal boundaries, but also already overseas. All this, however, was still very undeveloped; the precious metals were beginning to be the predominant and general money commodity, but still uncoined, exchanging simply by their naked weight.

The distinction of rich and poor appears beside that of freemen and slaves – with the new division of labour, a new cleavage of society into classes. The inequalities of property among the individual heads of families break up the old communal household communities wherever they had still managed to survive, and with them the common cultivation of the soil by and for these communities. The cultivated land is allotted for use to single families, at first temporarily, later permanently. The transition to full private property is gradually accomplished, parallel with the transition of the pairing marriage into monogamy. The single family is becoming the economic unit of society.

The denser population necessitates closer consolidation both for internal and external action. The confederacy of related tribes becomes everywhere a necessity, and soon also their fusion involving the fusion of the separate tribal territories into one territory of the nation. The military leader of the people – *rex, basileus, thiudans* – becomes an indispensable, permanent official. The assembly of the people takes form wherever it did not already exist. Military leader, council, assembly of the people are the organs of gentile society developed into military democracy – military, since war and organization for war have now become regular functions of national life. Their neighbours' wealth excites the greed of peoples who already see in the acquisition of wealth one of the main aims of life. They are barbarians; they think it easier and in fact more honourable to get riches by pillage than by work. War, formerly waged only in revenge for injuries or to extend territory that had grown too small, is now waged simply for plunder and becomes a regular industry. Not without reason the bristling battlements stand menacingly about the new fortified towns; in the moat at their foot yawns the grave of the gentile constitution, and already they rear their towers into civilization. Similarly in the interior, the wars of plunder increase the power of the supreme military leader and the subordinate commanders; the customary election of their successors from the same families is gradually transformed, especially after the introduction of father right, into a right of hereditary succession, first tolerated, then claimed, finally usurped; the foundation of the hereditary monarchy and the hereditary nobility is laid. Thus the organs of the gentile constitution gradually tear themselves loose from their roots in the people, in gens, phratry, tribe, and the whole gentile constitution changes into its opposite: from an organization of tribes for the free ordering of their own affairs it becomes an organization for the plundering and oppression of their neighbours; and correspondingly its organs change from instruments of the will of the people into independent organs for the domination and oppression of the people. That, however, would never have been possible if the greed for riches had not split the members of the gens into rich and poor, if 'the property differences within one and the same gens had not transformed its unity of interest into antagonism between its members' (Marx), if the extension of slavery had not already begun to make working for a living seem fit only for slaves and more dishonourable than pillage.

We have now reached the threshold of civilization. Civilization opens with a new advance in the division of labour. At the lowest stage of barbarism men produced only directly for their own needs; any acts of exchange were isolated occurrences, the object of exchange merely some fortuitous surplus.

In the middle stage of barbarism we already find among the pastoral peoples a possession in the form of cattle which, once the herd has attained a certain size, regularly produces a surplus over and above the tribe's own requirements, leading to a division of labour between pastoral peoples and backward tribes without herds, and hence to the existence of two different levels of production side by side with one another and to the conditions necessary for regular exchange. The upper stage of barbarism brings us the further division of labour between agriculture and handicrafts, hence the production of a continually increasing portion of the products of labour directly for exchange, so that exchange between individual producers assumes the importance of a vital social function. Civilization consolidates and intensifies all these existing divisions of labour, particularly by sharpening the opposition between town and country (the town may economically dominate the country, as in antiquity, or the country the town, as in the Middle Ages), and it adds a third division of labour peculiar to itself and of decisive importance. It creates a class which no longer concerns itself with production, but only with the exchange of the products – the *merchants*. Hitherto whenever classes had begun to form, it had always been exclusively in the field of production; the persons engaged in production were separated into those who directed and those who executed or else into large-scale and small-scale producers. Now for the first time a class appears which, without in any way participating in production, captures the direction of production as a whole and economically subjugates the producers; which makes itself into an indispensable middleman between any two producers and exploits them both. Under the pretext that they save the producers the trouble and risk of exchange, extend the sale of their products to distant markets and are therefore the most useful class of the population, a class of parasites comes into being, genuine social sycophants, who, as a reward for their actually very insignificant services, skim all the cream off production at home and abroad, rapidly amass enormous wealth and a corresponding social influence, and for that reason receive under civilization ever higher honours and ever greater control of production until at last they also bring forth a product of their own – the periodical trade crises.

At our stage of development, however, the young merchants had not even begun to dream of the great destiny awaiting them. But they were growing and making themselves indispensable, which was quite sufficient. And with the formation of the merchant class came also the development of *metallic money*, the minted coin, a new instrument for the domination of the non-producer over the producer and his production. The commodity of commodities had been discovered, that which holds all other commodities hidden in itself, the magic power which can change at will into everything desirable and desired. The man who had it ruled the world of production, and who had more of it than anybody else? – the merchant. The worship of money was safe in his hands. He took good care to make it clear that, in face of money, all commodities and hence all producers of commodities must prostrate themselves in adoration in the dust. He proved practically that all other forms of wealth fade into mere semblance beside this incarnation of wealth as such. Never again has the power of money shown itself in such primitive brutality and violence as during these days of its youth. After commodities had begun to sell for money, loans and advances in money came also, and with them interest and usury. No legislation of later times so utterly and ruthlessly delivers over the debtor to the usurious creditor as the legislation of ancient Athens and ancient Rome – and in both cities it rose spontaneously as customary law without any compulsion other than the economic.

Alongside wealth in commodities and slaves, alongside wealth in money, there now appeared wealth in land also. The individuals' rights of possession in the pieces of land originally allotted to them by gens or tribe had now become so established that the land was their hereditary property. Recently they had striven above all to secure their freedom against the rights of the gentile community over these lands since these rights had become for them a fetter. They got rid of the fetter – but soon afterwards of their new landed property also. Full, free ownership of the land meant not only power, uncurtailed and unlimited, to possess the land; it meant also the power to alienate it. As long as the land belonged to the gens, no such power could exist. But when the new landed proprietor shook off once and for all the fetters laid upon him by the prior right of gens and tribe, he also cut the ties which had hitherto inseparably attached him to the land. Money, invented at the same time as private property in land, showed him what that meant. Land could now become a commodity; it could be sold and pledged. Scarcely had private property in land been introduced than the mortgage was already invented (*see* Athens). As hetaerism and prostitution dog the heels of monogamy, so from now onward mortgage dogs the heels of private land ownership. You asked for full, free alienable ownership of the land and now you have got it – '*tu l'as voulu, Georges Dandin.*'

With trade expansion, money and usury, private property in land and mortgages, the concentration and centralization of wealth in the hands of a small class rapidly advanced, accompanied by an increasing impoverishment of the masses and an increasing mass of impoverishment. The new aristocracy of wealth, in so far as it had not been identical from the outset with the old hereditary aristocracy, pushed it permanently into the background (in Athens, in Rome, among the Germans). And simultaneous with this division of the citizens into classes according to wealth, there was an enormous increase, particularly in Greece, in the number of slaves* whose forced labour was the foundation on which the superstructure of the entire society was reared.

Let us now see what had become of the gentile constitution in this social upheaval. Confronted by the new forces in whose growth it had had no share, the gentile constitution was helpless. The necessary condition for its existence was

* For the number of slaves in Athens, *see* above, p. 153. In Corinth at the height of its power, the number of slaves was 460,000, in Aegina, 470,000 – in both cases, ten times the population of free citizens.

that the members of a gens or at least of a tribe were settled together in the same territory and were its sole inhabitants. That had long ceased to be the case. Every territory now had a heterogeneous population belonging to the most varied gentes and tribes; everywhere slaves, protected persons and aliens lived side by side with citizens. The settled conditions of life which had only been achieved towards the end of the middle stage of barbarism were broken up by the repeated shifting and changing of residence under the pressure of trade, alteration of occupation and changes in the ownership of the land. The members of the gentile bodies could no longer meet to look after their common concerns; only unimportant matters, like the religious festivals, were still perfunctorily attended to. In addition to the needs and interests with which the gentile bodies were intended and fitted to deal, the upheaval in productive relations and the resulting change in the social structure had given rise to new needs and interests which were not only alien to the old gentile order, but ran directly counter to it at every point. The interests of the groups of handicraftsmen which had arisen with the division of labour, the special needs of the town as opposed to the country, called for new organs. But each of these groups was composed of people of the most diverse gentes, phratries, and tribes, and even included aliens. Such organs had therefore to be formed outside the gentile constitution, alongside of it, and hence in opposition to it. And this conflict of interests was at work within every gentile body, appearing in its most extreme form in the association of rich and poor, usurers and debtors, in the same gens and the same tribe. Further, there was the new mass of population outside the gentile bodies, which, as in Rome, was able to become a power in the land and at the same time was too numerous to be gradually absorbed into the kinship groups and tribes. In relation to this mass, the gentile bodies stood opposed as closed, privileged corporations; the primitive natural democracy had changed into a malign aristocracy. Lastly, the gentile constitution had grown out of a society which knew no internal contradictions, and it was only adapted to such a society. It possessed no means of coercion except public opinion. But here was a society which by all its economic conditions of life had been forced to split itself into freemen and slaves, into the exploiting rich and the exploited poor; a society which not only could never again reconcile these contradictions, but was compelled always to intensify them. Such a society could only exist either in the continuous open fight of these classes against one another or else under the rule of a third power, which, apparently standing above the warring classes, suppressed their open conflict and allowed the class struggle to be fought out at most in the economic field, in so-called legal form. The gentile constitution was finished. It had been shattered by the division of labour and its result, the cleavage of society into classes. It was replaced by the *state*.

The three main forms in which the state arises on the ruins of the gentile constitution have been examined in detail above. Athens provides the purest, classic form; here the state springs directly and mainly out of the class oppositions which develop within gentile society itself. In Rome, gentile society becomes a closed aristocracy in the midst of the numerous *plebs* who stand outside it and have duties but no rights; the victory of *plebs* breaks up the old constitution based on kinship and erects on its ruins the state, into which both the gentile aristocracy and the *plebs* are soon completely absorbed. Lastly, in the case of the German conquerors of the Roman Empire, the state springs directly out of the conquest of large foreign territories which the gentile constitution provides no means of governing. But because this conquest involves neither a serious struggle with the original population nor a more advanced division of labour; because conquerors and conquered are almost on the same level of economic development, and the economic basis of society remains therefore as before – for these reasons the gentile constitution is able to survive for many centuries in the altered, territorial form of the mark constitution and even for a time to rejuvenate itself in a feebler shape in the later noble and patrician families, and indeed in peasant families, as in Ditmarschen.*

The state is therefore by no means a power imposed on society from without; just as little is it 'the reality of the moral idea', 'the image and the reality of reason', as Hegel maintains. Rather, it is a product of society at a particular stage of development; it is the admission that this society has involved itself in insoluble self-contradiction and is cleft into irreconcilable antagonisms which it is powerless to exorcize. But in order that these antagonisms, classes with conflicting economic interest, shall not consume themselves and society in fruitless struggle, a power, apparently standing above society, has become necessary to moderate the conflict and keep it within the bounds of 'order'; and this power, arisen out of society but placing itself above it and increasingly alienating itself from it, is the state.

In contrast to the old gentile organization, the state is distinguished firstly by the grouping of its members *on a territorial basis*. The old gentile bodies, formed and held together by ties of blood had, as we have seen, become inadequate largely because they presupposed that the gentile members were bound to one particular locality, whereas this had long ago ceased to be the case. The territory was still there, but the people had become mobile. The territorial division was therefore taken as the starting point and the system introduced by which citizens exercised their public rights and duties where they took up residence, without regard to gens or tribe. This organization of the citizens of the state according to domicile is common to all states. To us, therefore, this organization seems natural; but, as we have seen, hard and protracted struggles were necessary before it was able in Athens and Rome to displace the old organization founded on kinship.

The second distinguishing characteristic is the institution

* The first historian who had at any rate an approximate conception of the nature of the gens was Niebuhr, and for this he had to thank his acquaintance with the Ditmarschen families, though he was overhasty in transferring their characteristics to the gens.

of a *public force* which is no longer immediately identical with the people's own organization of themselves as an armed power. This special public force is needed because a self-acting armed organization of the people has become impossible since their cleavage into classes. The slaves also belong to the population; as against the 365,000 slaves, the 90,000 Athenian citizens constitute only a privileged class. The people's army of the Athenian democracy confronted the slaves as an aristocratic public force and kept them in check; but to keep the citizens in check as well, a police force was needed as described above. This public force exists in every state; it consists not merely of armed men but also of material appendages, prisons and coercive institutions of all kinds, of which gentile society knew nothing. It may be very insignificant, practically negligible, in societies with still undeveloped class antagonisms and living in remote areas, as at times and in places in the United States of America. But it becomes stronger in proportion as the class antagonisms within the state become sharper and as adjoining states grow larger and more populous. It is enough to look at Europe today, where class struggle and rivalry in conquest have brought the public power to such a pitch that it threatens to devour the whole of society and even the state itself.

In order to maintain this public power, contributions from the citizens are necessary – *taxes*. These were completely unknown to gentile society. We know more than enough about them today. With advancing civilization, even taxes are not sufficient; the state draws drafts on the future, contracts loans – *state debts*. Our old Europe can tell a tale about these, too.

In possession of the public power and the right of taxation, the officials now present themselves as organs of society standing *above* society. The free, willing respect accorded to the organs of the gentile constitution is not enough for them, even if they could have it. Representatives of a power which estranges them from society, they have to be given prestige by means of special decrees which invest them with a peculiar sanctity and inviolability. The lowest police officer of the civilized state has more 'authority' than all the organs of gentile society put together; but the mightiest prince and the greatest statesman or general of civilization might envy the humblest of the gentile chiefs, the unforced and unquestioned respect accorded to him. For the one stands in the midst of society; the other is forced to pose as something outside and above it.

As the state arose from the need to keep class antagonisms in check, but also arose in the thick of the fight between the classes, it is normally the state of the most powerful, economically dominant class, which by its means becomes also the politically dominant class and so acquires new means of holding down and exploiting the oppressed class. The ancient state was, above all, the state of the slave owners for holding down the slaves, just as the feudal state was the organ of the nobility for holding down the peasant serfs and bondsmen, and the modern representative state is an instrument for exploiting wage labour by capital. Exceptional periods, however, occur when the warring classes are so nearly equal in forces that the state power, as apparent mediator, acquires for the moment a certain independence in relation to both. This applies to the absolute monarchy of the seventeenth and eighteenth centuries, which balanced the nobility and the bourgeoisie against one another, and to the Bonapartism of the First and particularly of the Second French Empire, which played off the proletariat against the bourgeoisie and the bourgeoisie against the proletariat. The latest achievement in this line, in which ruler and ruled look equally comic, is the new German Empire of the Bismarckian nation; here the capitalists and the workers are balanced against one another and both of them fleeced for the benefit of the decayed Prussian cabbage Junkers.

Further, in most historical states the rights conceded to citizens are graded on a property basis whereby it is directly admitted that the state is an organization for the protection of the possessing class against the non-possessing class. This is already the case in the Athenian and Roman property classes; similarly in the medieval feudal state in which the extent of political power was determined by the extent of land-ownership; similarly, also, in the electoral qualifications in modern parliamentary states. This political recognition of property differences is, however, by no means essential. On the contrary, it marks a low stage in the development of the state. The highest form of the state, the democratic republic, which in our modern social conditions becomes more and more an unavoidable necessity and is the form of state in which alone the last decisive battle between proletariat and bourgeoisie can be fought out – the democratic republic no longer officially recognizes differences of property. Wealth here employs its power indirectly, but all the more surely. It does this in two ways: by plain corruption of officials, of which America is the classic example; and by an alliance between the government and the stock exchange, which is effected all the more easily the higher the state debt mounts and the more the joint-stock companies concentrate in their hands not only transport but also production itself, and themselves have their own centre in the stock exchange. In addition to America, the latest French republic illustrates this strikingly, and honest little Switzerland has also given a creditable performance in this field. But that a democratic republic is not essential to this brotherly bond between government and stock exchange is proved not only by England but also by the new German Empire, where it is difficult to say who scored most by the introduction of universal suffrage, Bismarck or the Bleichröder bank. And lastly the possessing class rules directly by means of universal suffrage. As long as the oppressed class – in our case, therefore, the proletariat – is not yet ripe for its self-liberation, so long will it in its majority recognize the existing order of society as the only possible one and remain politically the tail of the capitalist class, its extreme left wing. But in the measure in which it matures toward its self-emancipation, in the same measure it constitutes itself as its own party and votes for its own representatives, not those of the capitalists. Universal suffrage is thus the gauge of the maturity of the working class. It cannot and never will be anything more in the modern state; but that is enough. On the day when the thermometer of universal suffrage shows boiling point among the workers, they as well as the capitalists will know where they stand.

The state, therefore, has not existed from all eternity. There have been societies which have managed without it, which had no notion of the state or state power. At a definite stage of economic development, which necessarily involved the cleavage of society into classes, the state became a necessity because of this cleavage. We are now rapidly approaching a stage in the development of production at which the existence of these classes has not only ceased to be a necessity but becomes a positive hindrance to production. They will fall as inevitably as they once arose. The state inevitably falls with them. The society which organizes production anew on the basis of free and equal association of the producers will put the whole state machinery where it will then belong – into the museum of antiquities, next to the spinning wheel and the bronze axe.

Civilization is, therefore, according to the above analysis, the stage of development in society at which the division of labour, the exchange between individuals arising from it, and the commodity production which combines them both come to their full growth and revolutionize the whole of previous society.

At all earlier stages of society, production was essentially collective, just as consumption proceeded by direct distribution of the products within larger or smaller communistic communities. This collective production was very limited; but inherent in it was the producers' control over their process of production and their product. They knew what became of their product: they consumed it; it did not leave their hands. And so long as production remains on this basis, it cannot grow above the heads of the producers nor raise up incorporeal alien powers against them, as in civilization is always and inevitably the case.

But the division of labour slowly insinuates itself into this process of production. It undermines the collectivity of production and appropriation, elevates appropriation by individuals into the general rule, and thus creates exchange between individuals – how it does so, we have examined above. Gradually commodity production becomes the dominating form.

With commodity production, production no longer for use by the producers but for exchange, the products necessarily change hands. In exchanging his product, the producer surrenders it; he no longer knows what becomes of it. When money, and with money the merchant, steps in as intermediary between the producers, the process of exchange becomes still more complicated, the final fate of the products still more uncertain. The merchants are numerous, and none of them knows what the other is doing. The commodities already pass not only from hand to hand; they also pass from market to market; the producers have lost control over the total production within their own spheres, and the merchants have not gained it. Products and production become subjects of chance.

But chance is only the one pole of a relation whose other pole is named 'necessity'. In the world of nature where chance also seems to rule, we have long since demonstrated in each separate field the inner necessity and law asserting itself in this chance. But what is true of the natural world is true also of society. The more a social activity, a series of social processes, becomes too powerful for men's conscious control and grows above their heads, and the more it appears a matter of pure chance, then all the more surely within this chance the laws peculiar to it and inherent in it assert themselves as if by natural necessity. Such laws also govern the chances of commodity production and exchange. To the individuals producing or exchanging, they appear as alien, at first often unrecognized, powers, whose nature must first be laboriously investigated and established. These economic laws of commodity production are modified with the various stages of this form of production; but in general the whole period of civilization is dominated by them. And still to this day the product rules the producer; still to this day the total production of society is regulated, not by a jointly devised plan, but by blind laws which manifest themselves with elemental violence in the final instance in the storms of the periodical trade crises.

We saw above how at a fairly early stage in the development of production, human labour power obtains the capacity of producing a considerably greater product than is required for the maintenance of the producers, and how this stage of development was in the main the same as that in which division of labour and exchange between individuals arises. It was not long then before the great 'truth' was discovered that man also can be a commodity, that human energy can be exchanged and put to use by making a man into a slave. Hardly had men begun to exchange than already they themselves were being exchanged. The active became the passive, whether the men liked it or not.

With slavery, which attained its fullest development under civilization, came the first great cleavage of society into an exploiting and an exploited class. This cleavage persisted during the whole civilized period. Slavery is the first form of exploitation, the form peculiar to the ancient world; it is succeeded by serfdom in the Middle Ages and wage labour in the more recent period. These are the three great forms of servitude characteristic of the three great epochs of civilization; open, and in recent times disguised, slavery always accompanies them.

The stage of commodity production with which civilization begins is distinguished economically by the introduction of (1) metal money and with it money capital, interest and usury, (2) merchants as the class of intermediaries between the producers, (3) private ownership of land and the mortgage system, (4) slave labour as the dominant form of production. The form of family corresponding to civilization and coming to definite supremacy with it is monogamy, the domination of the man over the woman and the single family as the economic unit of society. The central link in civilized society is the state, which in all typical periods is without exception the state of the ruling class and in all cases continues to be essentially a machine for holding down the oppressed, exploited class. Also characteristic of civilization is the establishment of a permanent opposition between town and country as the basis of the whole social division of labour; and further, the introduction of wills whereby the owner of property is still able to dispose over it even when he is dead. This institution, which is a direct affront to the old gentile constitution, was unknown in Athens until the time of Solon; in Rome it was introduced early, though we do not know the date;* among the Germans it was the clerics who introduced it in order that there might be nothing to stop the pious German from leaving his legacy to the Church.

With this as its basic constitution, civilization achieved things of which gentile society was not even remotely capable. But it achieved them by setting in motion the lowest instincts and passions in man and developing them at the expense of all his other abilities. From its first day to this, sheer greed was the driving spirit of civilization; wealth and again wealth and once more wealth, wealth, not of society but of the single scurvy individual – here was its one and final aim. If at the same time the progressive development of science and a repeated flowering of supreme art dropped into its lap, it was only because without them modern wealth could not have completely realized its achievements.

Since civilization is founded on the exploitation of one class by another class, its whole development proceeds in a constant contradiction. Every step forward in production is

* The second part of Lassalle's *Das System der erworbenen Rechte* (*System of Acquired Rights*) turns chiefly on the proposition that the Roman testament is as old as Rome itself, that there was never in Roman history 'a time when there were no testaments', and that, on the contrary, the testament originated in pre-Roman times out of the cult of the dead. Lassalle, as a faithful Hegelian of the old school, derives the provisions of Roman law not from the social relations of the Romans but from the 'speculative concept' of the human will, and so arrives at this totally unhistorical conclusion. This is not to be wondered at in a book which comes to the conclusion, on the ground of the same speculative concept, that the transfer of property was a purely secondary matter in Roman inheritance. Lassalle not only believes in the illusions of the Roman jurists, particularly of the earlier periods; he outdoes them.

at the same time a step backward in the position of the oppressed class, that is, of the great majority. Whatever benefits some necessarily injures the others; every fresh emancipation of one class is necessarily a new oppression for another class. The most striking proof of this is provided by the introduction of machinery, the effects of which are now known to the whole world. And if among the barbarians, as we saw, the distinction between rights and duties could hardly be drawn, civilization makes the difference and antagonism between them clear even to the dullest intelligence by giving one class practically all the rights and the other class practically all the duties.

But that should not be; what is good for the ruling class must also be good for the whole of society with which the ruling class identifies itself. Therefore the more civilization advances, the more it is compelled to cover the evils it necessarily creates with the cloak of love and charity, to palliate them or to deny them – in short, to introduce a conventional hypocrisy which was unknown to earlier forms of society and even to the first stages of civilization, and which culminates in the pronouncement: the exploitation of the oppressed class is carried on by the exploiting class simply and solely in the interests of the exploited class itself; and if the exploited class cannot see it and even grows rebellious, that is the basest ingratitude to its benefactors, the exploiters.*

And now, in conclusion, Morgan's judgement of civilization:

Since the advent of civilization, the outgrowth of property has been so immense, its forms so diversified, its uses so expanding and

* I originally intended to place the brilliant criticism of civilization which is found scattered through the work of Charles Fourier beside that of Morgan and my own. Unfortunately, I have not the time. I will only observe that Fourier already regards monogamy and private property in land as the chief characteristics of civilization, and that he calls civilization a war of the rich against the poor. We also find already in his work the profound recognition that in all societies which are imperfect and split into antagonisms single families (*les familles incohérentes*) are the economic units.

its management so intelligent in the interests of its owners, that it has become, on the part of the people, *an unmanageable power. The human mind stands bewildered in the presence of its own creation.* The time will come, nevertheless, when human intelligence will rise to the mastery over property, and define the relations of the state to the property it protects, as well as the obligations and the limits of the rights of its owners. The interests of society are paramount to individual interests, and the two must be brought into just and harmonious relations. A mere property career is not the final destiny of mankind, if progress is to be the law of the future as it has been of the past. The time which has passed away since civilization began is but a fragment of the past duration of man's existence; and but a fragment of the ages yet to come. The dissolution of society bids fair to become the termination of a career of which property is the end and aim; because such a career contains the elements of self-destruction. Democracy in government, brotherhood in society, equality in rights and privileges, and universal education, foreshadow the next higher plane of society to which experience, intelligence and knowledge are steadily tending. *It will be a revival, in a higher form, of the liberty, equality and fraternity of the ancient gentes* [pp. 561–2; Engels's italics].

A Recently Discovered Case of Group Marriage

Since it has recently become fashionable among certain rationalistic ethnographers to deny the existence of group marriage, the following report is of interest; I translate it from the *Russkiye Vyedomosti*, Moscow, 14 October 1892 (Old Style). Not only group marriage, i.e., the right of mutual sexual intercourse between a number of men and a number of women, is expressly affirmed to be in full force, but a form of group marriage which closely follows the punaluan marriage of the Hawaiians, the most developed and classic phase of group marriage. While the typical punaluan family consists of a number of brothers (own and collateral) who are married to a number of own and collateral sisters, we here find on the island of Sakhalin that a man is married to all the wives of his brothers and to all the sisters of his wife, which means, seen from the woman's side, that his wife may freely practise sexual intercourse with the brothers of her husband and the husbands of her sisters. It therefore differs from the typical form of punaluan marriage only in the fact that the brothers of the husband and the husbands of the sisters are not necessarily the same persons.

It should further be observed that this report again confirms what I said in *The Origin of the Family*, 4th edition [see p. 75]: group marriage does not look at all like what our brothel-obsessed philistine imagines. The partners in group marriage do not lead in public the same kind of lascivious life as he practises in secret, but this form of marriage, at least in the instances still known to occur today, differs in practice from a loose pairing marriage or from polygamy only in the fact that custom permits sexual intercourse in a number of cases where otherwise it would be severely punished. That the actual exercise of these rights is gradually dying out only proves that this form of marriage is itself destined to die out, which is further confirmed by its infrequency.

The whole description, moreover, is interesting because it again demonstrates the similarity, even the identity in their main characteristics, of the social institutions of primitive peoples at approximately the same stage of development. Most of what the report states about these Mongoloids on the island of Sakhalin also holds for the Dravidian tribes of India, the South Sea Islanders at the time of their discovery, and the American Indians. The report runs:

'At the session of 10 October (Old Style; 22 October, New Style) of the Anthropological Section of the Society of the Friends of Natural Science, N. A. Yanchuk read an interesting communication from Mr [Lev J.] Sternberg on the Gilyaks, a little-studied tribe on the island of Sakhalin, who are at the cultural level of savagery. The Gilyaks are acquainted neither with agriculture nor with pottery; they procure their food chiefly by hunting and fishing; they warm water in wooden vessels by throwing in heated stones, etc. Of particular interest are their institutions relating to the family and to the gens. The Gilyak addresses as father, not only his own natural father, but also all the brothers of his father; all the wives of these brothers, as well as all the sisters of his mother, he addresses as his mothers; the children of all these "fathers" and "mothers" he addresses as his brothers and sisters. This system of address also exists, as is well known, among the Iroquois and other Indian tribes of North America, as also among some tribes of India. But whereas in these cases it has long since ceased to correspond to the actual conditions, among the Gilyaks it serves to designate *a state still valid today*. To this day *every Gilyak has the rights of a husband in regard to the wives of his brothers and to the sisters of his wife*; at any rate, the exercise of these rights is not regarded as impermissible. These survivals of group marriage on the basis of the gens are reminiscent of the well-known punaluan marriage which still existed in the Sandwich Islands in the first half of this century. Family and gens relations of this type form the basis of the whole gentile order and social constitution of the Gilyaks.

'The gens of a Gilyak consists of all – nearer and more remote, real and nominal – brothers of his father, of their fathers and mothers (?), of the children of his brothers, and of his own children. One can readily understand that a gens so constituted may comprise an enormous number of people. Life within the gens proceeds according to the following principles. Marriage within the gens is unconditionally prohibited. When a Gilyak dies, his wife passes by decision of the gens to one of his brothers, own or nominal. The gens provides for the maintenance of all of its members who are unable to work. "We have no poor," said a Gilyak to the writer. "Whoever is in need, is fed by the *khal* [gens]." The members of the gens are further united by common sacrificial ceremonies and festivals, a common burial place, etc.

'The gens guarantees the life and security of its members against attacks by non-gentiles; the means of repression used is blood revenge, though under Russian rule the practice has very much declined. Women are completely excepted from gentile blood revenge. In some very rare cases the gens adopts members of other gentes. It is a general rule that the property of a deceased member may not pass out of the gens; in this respect the famous provision of the Twelve Tables holds literally among the Gilyaks: *si suos heredes non habet, gentiles familiam habento* – if he has no heirs of his own, the members of the gens shall inherit. No important event takes place in the life of a Gilyak without participation by the gens. Not very long ago, about one or two generations, the oldest gentile member was the head of the community, the *starosta* of the gens; today the functions of the chief elder of the gens are restricted almost solely to presiding over religious ceremonies. The gentes are often dispersed among widely distant places, but even when separated the members of a gens still remember one another and continue to give one another hospitality, and to provide mutual assistance and protection, etc. Except under the most extreme necessity, the Gilyak never leaves the fellow members of his gens or the graves of his gens. Gentile society has impressed a very definite stamp on the whole mental life of the Gilyaks, on their character, their customs and institutions. The habit of common discussion and decision on all matters, the necessity of continually taking an active part in all questions affecting the members of the gens, the solidarity of blood revenge, the fact of being compelled and accustomed to live together with ten or more like himself in great tents (*yurtas*), and, in short, to be always with other people – all this has given the Gilyak a sociable and open character. The Gilyak is extraordinarily hospitable; he loves to entertain guests and to come himself as a guest. This admirable habit of hospitality is especially prominent in times of distress. In a bad year, when a Gilyak has nothing for himself or for his dogs to eat, he does not stretch out his hand for alms, but confidently seeks hospitality, and is fed, often for a considerable time.

'Among the Gilyaks of Sakhalin crimes from motives of personal gain practically never occur. The Gilyak keeps his valuables in a storehouse, which is never locked. He has such a keen sense of shame that if he is convicted of a disgraceful act, he immediately goes into the forest and hangs himself. Murder is very rare, and is hardly ever committed except in anger, never from intentions of gain. In his dealings with other people, the Gilyak shows himself honest, reliable, and conscientious.

'Despite their long subjection to the Manchurians, now become Chinese, and despite the corrupting influence of the settlement of the Amur district, the Gilyaks still preserve in their moral character many of the virtues of a primitive tribe. But the fate awaiting their social order cannot be averted. One or two more generations, and the Gilyaks on the mainland will have been completely Russianized, and together with the benefits of culture they will also acquire its defects. The Gilyaks on the island of Sakhalin, being more or less remote from the centres of Russian settlement, have some prospect of preserving their way of life unspoiled rather longer. But among them, too, the influence of their Russian neighbours is beginning to make itself felt. The Gilyaks come into the villages to trade, they go to Nikolaievsk to look for work; and every Gilyak who returns from such work to his home brings with him the same atmosphere which the Russian worker takes back from the town into his village. And at the same time, working in the town, with its chances and changes of fortune, destroys more and more that primitive equality which is such a prominent feature of the artlessly simple economic life of these peoples.

'Mr Sternberg's article, which also contains information about their religious views and customs and their legal institutions, will appear unabridged in the *Etnografitcheskoye Obozrenie* (*Ethnographical Review*).'

Glossary of Some Contemporary Terms and Concordance with Engels's Usage

BRIDE-PRICE: Food, cloth, cattle, or other goods given by kinsmen of the bridegroom to the family of the bride, referred to by Engels as 'gift payments' (p. 78).

CROSS-COUSINS: Children of siblings of the opposite sex, i.e., children of one's mother's brother or one's father's sister. Children of siblings of the same sex are called parallel cousins. When descent is 'unilineal', or counted on one side only, and marriage is 'exogamous', or outside of the kin group, cross-cousins are outside of one's clan and are very commonly preferred marriage partners. Hence Engels's discussion, pp. 70, 74.

ENDOGAMY: Marriage within the defined group – lineage, clan, village, etc. Castes are by definition endogamous; classes tend to be so.

EXOGAMY: Marriage outside the defined group. Clans and lineages are typically exogamous.

GENS: A group of actual and fictive kinsmen related through one parental line only. The term most commonly used today is 'clan'. Matrilineal lines trace relationship through the mother, patrilineal through the father. Bilateral clans are presumably transitional. All clan members are theoretically descendants of a common ancestor. Sections of the clan that can directly trace their relationships are usually referred to as lineages. Another term for a unilineal descent group, though not in common use, is 'sib'.

HAWAIIAN SYSTEM: A form of kin terminology in which siblings and cousins of the same sex are all referred to by the same term. The system is common in the Pacific Islands and in the Americas, although with variants in the terms used for aunts and uncles. The study of kinship terminologies and their many variations has become highly specialized with regard to typology; more needs to be done, however, on the changes that take place within them under the impact of colonialism.

MATRILOCALITY: Residence of a newly married couple with the parents of the woman, by contrast with patrilocality, or residence with the parents of the man. Temporary matrilocality is often followed by patrilocality. Residence may also be 'neolocal'.

MOIETY: A division of a society into two groups, generally unilineal and exogamous. A moiety may subsume several clans.

MOTHER RIGHT: Descent reckoned through the mother, now referred to as 'matrilineality'. 'Patrilineal' descent is reckoned through the father. Our descent system is 'bilateral'. The notion of 'matriarchy', or rule by women, as accompanying matrilineal descent is specifically contradicted by Engels. He writes: 'To denote this exclusive recognition of descent through the mother and the relations of inheritance which in time resulted from it, he [Bachofen] uses the term "mother right", which for the sake of brevity I retain. The term is, however, ill-chosen, since at this stage of society [primitive communism] there cannot yet be any talk of "right" in the legal sense' (pp. 71–2).

POLYGAMY, POLYGYNY, POLYANDRY: Forms of plural marriage. Polygamy is the inclusive term, although it may often be used to denote 'polygyny' or plural wives. Polyandry refers to plural husbands.

PRIMITIVE: The term for peoples living in a hunting and gathering, or horticultural, economy is awkward due to its negative connotations in popular use. Suffice it to say, as Engels's book documents so thoroughly, primitive peoples are more 'civilized' than more 'advanced' societies if the term is used to denote humanistic interpersonal relations.

TRIBE: The term generally used for groups who share a common language and culture, but who do not constitute historically evolved 'nations'. The term has been too loosely used, however. It has been applied alike to societies which are no more than a loose aggregate of autonomous villages and to societies where there is a relatively centralized administrative and judicial apparatus. In many cases the development of formal tribal chieftainship has taken place as part of the struggle against colonial domination. The history of many North American Indian peoples exemplifies a transition from a more informal, to a 'tribal', and then 'national' organization and orientation.

Index

Aaby, Peter, 14

Adoption, 85, 120, 133 156, 157

Adultery, 76, 77, 92–3, 97, 98, 101, 105–6, 108–9, 167, 174–5

Aeschylus (525–456 BC), 40–41, 93, 137, 138

Africa, 59, 130

Agassiz, J. Louis R. (1807–73), 81

Agriculture, 57; among the Athenians, 146, 147; in Roman Empire, 185–6; separation of handicraft from, 200–201, 203, 206

Alphabet, 55

American Indians: and gens, 195–6; and mother right and father right, 86–7; and treatment of prisoners, 84–5; confederation of, 126–30; council and military organization of, 124–5; gentile organization of, 116ff., 132; offices and religion of, 124; system of consanguinity among, 58, 69ff., 76ff.; see also Iroquois

Ammianus Marcellinus (330–400), 100, 125

Anacreon (6th century BC), 108

Ancestor, gentile, 117, 134–6

Animal mating and societies, 62ff.

Anthropoid apes, 62–3, 64

Anthropology, English school of, 13ff., 25, 38, 45, 48–9, 116

Archons, 133–4, 152

Aristides (535–467 BC), 150

Aristocracy: at beginning of civilization, 205ff.; during barbarism, 202; gentile, 138–9; in Athenian state, 140, 142ff., 150; German, 179–80, 188–9; Roman, 162

Aristophanes (450–335 BC), 94

Aristotle (384–322 BC), 140

Aryans and Semites, 54–5, 84, 89, 196–7

Asian mode of production, see Oriental mode of production

Assemblies: German, 179, 189; Greek, 137ff., 142, 149, 151–2; Iroquois, 120, 121, 124–5; Roman, 160ff.; Welsh, 168

Augustus (63 BC–AD 14), first Roman Emperor, 155, 183

227

FOR THE BEST IN PAPERBACKS, LOOK FOR THE 🐧

In every corner of the world, on every subject under the sun, Penguin represents quality and variety – the very best in publishing today.

For complete information about books available from Penguin – including Puffins, Penguin Classics and Arkana – and how to order them, write to us at the appropriate address below. Please note that for copyright reasons the selection of books varies from country to country.

In the United Kingdom: Please write to *Dept E.P., Penguin Books Ltd, Harmondsworth, Middlesex, UB7 0DA.*

If you have any difficulty in obtaining a title, please send your order with the correct money, plus ten per cent for postage and packaging, to *PO Box No 11, West Drayton, Middlesex*

In the United States: Please write to *Dept BA, Penguin, 299 Murray Hill Parkway, East Rutherford, New Jersey 07073*

In Canada: Please write to *Penguin Books Canada Ltd, 2801 John Street, Markham, Ontario L3R 1B4*

In Australia: Please write to the *Marketing Department, Penguin Books Australia Ltd, P.O. Box 257, Ringwood, Victoria 3134*

In New Zealand: Please write to the *Marketing Department, Penguin Books (NZ) Ltd, Private Bag, Takapuna, Auckland 9*

In India: Please write to *Penguin Overseas Ltd, 706 Eros Apartments, 56 Nehru Place, New Delhi, 110019*

In the Netherlands: Please write to *Penguin Books Netherlands B.V., Postbus 195, NL–1380AD Weesp*

In West Germany: Please write to *Penguin Books Ltd, Friedrichstrasse 10–12, D–6000 Frankfurt/Main 1*

In Spain: Please write to *Alhambra Longman S.A., Fernandez de la Hoz 9, E–28010 Madrid*

In Italy: Please write to *Penguin Italia s.r.l., Via Como 4, I-20096 Pioltello (Milano)*

In France: Please write to *Penguin Books Ltd, 39 Rue de Montmorency, F-75003 Paris*

In Japan: Please write to *Longman Penguin Japan Co Ltd, Yamaguchi Building, 2–12–9 Kanda Jimbocho, Chiyoda-Ku, Tokyo 101*

FOR THE BEST IN PAPERBACKS, LOOK FOR THE 🐧

PENGUIN CLASSICS

FOR THE BEST IN PAPERBACKS, LOOK FOR THE 🐧

PENGUIN CLASSICS